"Millions of people suffer from animal and insect phobias. Not only are the fears they experience distressing and in some cases disabling, but individuals who suffer from these phobias are often embarrassed to admit to the problem and thus never seek treatment, even though specific phobias are highly treatable. Antony and McCabe have provided a step-by-step treatment plan—the same one that would be used by a skilled clinician—that can be used by anyone to overcome their phobia in the privacy of their own home!"

—*William C. Sanderson, Ph.D., professor of psychology and director of the Anxiety and Depression Treatment Program at Hofstra University in Hempstead, NY*

"Animal and insect phobias are prevalent, and they often lead to major distress and impaired functioning in everyday life. In this self-help book, Antony and McCabe address these phobias head on. Their advice is clinically sensitive and based on the best scientific evidence available to us at this time. They show us how to confront our fears, change our dysfunctional thoughts, and overcome our avoidance. This is a much-needed book—one that every person who experiences these phobias should read, as should their therapists! It is a book whose time has come. Phobias beware!"

—*Thomas H. Ollendick, Ph.D., University Distinguished Professor of Psychology and director of the Child Study Center at the Virginia Polytechnic Institute and State University*

"Phobia specialists around the world use exposure therapy to help their patients because research has shown that it works. Antony and McCabe describe these same techniques in this straightforward guidebook filled with helpful tips and examples of people who have overcome severe fear of animals. This book is the place to start for phobia sufferers who are trying to conquer their fear on their own or with a caring helper or professional. It is also fascinating reading for the beginning therapist or for those who are simply interested in animal phobias."

> —*Sheila R. Woody, Ph.D., R.Psych., clinical faculty member in the Department of Psychology at the University of British Columbia*

overcoming animal & insect phobias

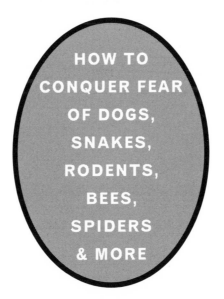

HOW TO CONQUER FEAR OF DOGS, SNAKES, RODENTS, BEES, SPIDERS & MORE

MARTIN M. ANTONY, PH.D.
RANDI E. MCCABE, PH.D.

New Harbinger Publications, Inc.

Distributed in Canada by Raincoast Books

Copyright © 2005 by Martin M. Antony and Randi E. McCabe
New Harbinger Publications, Inc.
5674 Shattuck Avenue
Oakland, CA 94609

Cover design by Amy Shoup
Acquired by Catharine Sutker
Text design by Tracy Marie Carlson

ISBN 1-57224-388-0 Paperback
Library of Congress Cataloging in Publication Data on file

Printed in the United States of America

New Harbinger Publications' Web site address: www.newharbinger.com

07   06   05

10   9   8   7   6   5   4   3   2   1

First printing

For Jacqui and Don Campbell
—M.M.A.

For Adelia and Angus
—R.E.M.

Contents

acknowledgments

We are grateful to Jennifer Harrington and Chris Watson for their comments and suggestions for improving the chapters of this book. Also, thanks to Peter Bieling, Michele Boivin, Mike Coons, Beth McConnell, Todd Murphy, Laura Summerfeldt, and Mark Watling for helping to expand upon our list of popular movies with animal scenes (chapter 4). Finally, thanks to Catharine Sutker, Carole Honeychurch, Brady Kahn, and everyone else at New Harbinger for their support. As always, they have been great to work with.

introduction

If you find yourself experiencing extreme fear when faced with certain kinds of animals, you should know that you are definitely not alone. Surveys of the general population have found that animals are among the most commonly feared situations or objects. For example, one study of more than eight thousand people in the United States found that 22.2 percent of individuals reported an intense fear of animals (Curtis et al. 1998)—a higher percentage than was found for any other feared situation (for example, heights, enclosed places, storms, or blood) asked about in the survey. Not only are animal fears common but a number of studies have found that people often fear more than one type of animal (Antony and Barlow 2002), making the problem even worse. After all, animals are all around us.

Most people are able to live with their fears, often by avoiding the animals that make them feel uncomfortable. If you are terrified of snakes but you never see snakes or even think about them, you really don't have a problem. However, for some individuals, the fear of animals is a significant concern. For example, Erin had an extreme fear of cats. She was constantly scanning her environment for cats, and she often avoided going for walks in her neighborhood for fear of seeing one. Occasionally, she was awoken by nightmares about cats, and she avoided visiting friends and family members who had them as pets. She was even nervous watching television and movies, because she never knew when a cat might appear. Clearly, Erin's fear was a problem for her. When a fear causes significant interference in your life, or when it is distressing for you to have the fear, the condition is considered a *phobia*. In one large survey (Curtis et al. 1998), 5.7 percent of individuals had a fear of animals that was severe enough to be called a phobia.

the purpose of this book

Although there are a number of books available on the topic of phobias, this is the first book to focus specifically on strategies for overcoming fears and phobias of animals. It is designed for individuals who have a fear of one or more animals or insects; it is also designed for their families. You may be able to use the strategies described in this book on your own. Alternatively, the techniques described in this book may work best for you when used under the supervision of an experienced therapist, or perhaps with a family member or friend who is able to work with you to overcome your phobia. Professionals who work with people who suffer from animal fears and phobias will also find this book useful.

the structure of this book

This book is organized into eight chapters. Chapters 1 and 2 provide information on the nature of animal phobias, including examples of typical animal phobias, research on the prevalence of animal phobias, a review of effective treatments, and theories regarding how animal phobias begin. Chapters 3 and 4 focus on strategies to prepare for treatment, including developing a hierarchy of feared situations, from most to least difficult to confront, finding the materials you need for treatment, and considering whether to seek professional help. Chapter 5 discusses exposure-based strategies for overcoming animal phobias. This chapter discusses the core of the treatment—if there is one chapter you read several times, it should be chapter 5 (we will return to this issue shortly). Chapter 6 discusses strategies for changing anxious thinking about animals, and chapter 7 will help you to develop a plan to maintain your improvements over time. Finally, chapter 8 is aimed at family members or friends who know someone with an animal phobia and who may be involved in helping that person overcome his or her fear.

how to use this book

We recommend that you read through the entire book initially, to obtain a broad overview of how the treatment works. As you work through chapters 1 through 4, you should complete the recommended exercises, which will prepare you for using the treatment strategies described in chapters 5 and 6. Once you have finished reading the entire book, return to chapters 5 and 6. We recommend that you read these chapters a second time and that you repeat the exercises (especially the exposure exercises in chapter 5) until your fear has decreased. Chapter 7 should be read again, after your fear has decreased and you are ready to consider strategies for staying well. Although the entire book may be of interest to family members or others who are helping someone work through his or her phobia, chapter 8 will be particularly useful for this purpose.

We recommend that you use a journal or notebook to complete the exercises throughout this book. In fact, don't bother reading any further until you have obtained your journal. Without practicing the various strategies described in the book, it is unlikely that you will notice a significant change in your fear. Keeping a journal will make it easier to keep up with the exercises.

can a self-help book really help?

Of all the different types of specific phobias that people have, animal phobias are the most thoroughly researched.

Procedures for overcoming animal phobias are well developed, and there is considerable evidence that severe fears of animals can be overcome fairly quickly for most individuals. In fact, in some studies, up to 90 percent of people with an animal phobia were able to overcome their fears in a single session lasting, on average, less than three hours (Öst 1989). Not only that, but most studies find that people who overcome their animal phobias are usually able to maintain their improvements over the long term (Öst 1996).

However, most of the research on treating animal phobias is based on treatment with a trained therapist. Only a small number of studies have investigated the use of self-help treatments for animal phobias, and all of these have been based on spider phobias. The few studies that have been conducted have had mixed results, but overall, treatment with a therapist tends to be more effective. Nevertheless, between 30 and 60 percent of people can achieve significant improvement with just a thirty-page self-help manual (Hellström and Öst 1995; Öst, Salkovskis, and Hellström 1991; Öst, Stridh, and Wolf 1998). Some people clearly can overcome their fears on their own.

Based on research by psychologist Lars-Göran Öst and his colleagues (Öst, Stridh, and Wolf 1998), the best predictors of whether you will benefit from self-help treatment for animal phobias include how motivated you are to improve and the extent to which the treatment makes sense to you (in other words, how credible or believable the manual seems). Here are a few variables that were found to play little or no role in predicting whether self-help treatment will succeed: the age at which your fear began, the number of years this fear has been present, whether there is a history of phobias in your family, and the severity of your phobia. So it doesn't matter how long you have had your fear or how severe it is. If you are motivated to conquer your fear and you follow the detailed suggestions outlined in this book, you have a good chance of overcoming your fear.

Although treatment is usually effective and brief, it is rarely easy. Treatment will require you to confront the animal you fear in a controlled, gradual way. In all likelihood, exposure to your feared animal will lead you to feel very uncomfortable and frightened. Initially, you may experience panicky feelings, crying, nightmares, and other unpleasant reactions. A decision to overcome your animal phobia must include a willingness to feel uncomfortable at the beginning of treatment for the purpose of eventually reaching a point where you can be around the animal with little or even no fear. Although the treatment is uncomfortable, this is something you can do.

Even if a self-help approach is not for you, this book may still be helpful. Understanding the nature of your fear and learning about the strategies that have proven to be useful for overcoming a fear of animals will help prepare you to eventually confront the problem. At the very least, the treatment strategies described in this book are effective for almost everyone, when used with a therapist. If you want to overcome your fear, there is no reason why you can't do it.

about animal phobias

Animal fears are the most frequently reported fears in the general population. Though the most commonly feared animals include creepy, crawly creatures, such as snakes, spiders, rodents, and bugs, other animals that are often feared include dogs, cats, birds, and bees. In fact, people can have a fear of just about any animal. For example, we have seen people with specific fears of worms, moths, squirrels, fish, cockroaches, ants, sharks, and owls. Many animal phobias have "official" names based on their Latin and Greek roots, though in practice these names are rarely used by people, including even researchers and professionals who work with people who have phobias. In other words, a phobia of spiders is usually just called a "spider phobia," rather than by its medical name, *arachnophobia*. Still, for the sake of interest, below is a list of twenty-five documented animal phobias and their medical names.

proper medical names for various animal phobias

The following list of animal phobias comes from www.phobialist.com:

amphibians (for example, frogs, newts, salamanders)—batrachophobia

animals—zoophobia

ants—myrmecophobia

bees—apiphobia or melissophobia

birds—ornithophobia

cats—ailurophobia, elurophobia, galeophobia, or gatophobia

chickens—alektorophobia

dogs (or rabies)—cynophobia

fish—ichthyophobia

frogs—ranidaphobia

horses—equinophobia or hippophobia

insects—entomophobia or insectophobia

mice—musophobia or murophobia

moths—mottephobia

otters—lutraphobia

reptiles (or creepy, crawly things)—herpetophobia

sharks—selachophobia

shellfish—ostraconophobia

snakes—ophidiophobia or snakephobia

spiders—arachnephobia or arachnophobia

termites—isopterophobia

toads—bufonophobia

wasps—spheksophobia

wild animals—agrizoophobia

worms—scoleciphobia

what is an animal phobia?

Nearly one in four people reports a fear of at least one animal. In fact, it is perfectly normal to be uncomfortable around dogs, snakes, bees, or other animals. Most of the time, having such a fear doesn't really get in the way of life, and it doesn't cause much distress or concern. Encounters with a feared animal may be infrequent, the level of fear may be mild, the fear may not impact upon a person's day-to-day life, and treatment is unnecessary. Such cases would not be referred to as animal *phobias*. Rather, we would describe these as *fears* of animals.

The term *animal phobia* refers to a specific type of anxiety disorder known as a *specific phobia* (American Psychiatric Association 2000). A specific phobia is an excessive or unrealistic fear of a specific object or situation, such as an animal or insect, heights, driving, flying, storms, enclosed places, the sight of blood, or getting an injection. The terms *excessive* and *unrealistic* mean that the fear is extreme and out of proportion to the actual risk in the situation (though there may really be a small risk of danger). In addition, the term *phobia* implies that the fear is severe enough to cause considerable impairment in a person's life (it must interfere with work, home life, relationships, hobbies, or other areas of functioning), or significant distress (in other words, it deeply bothers the person that he or she has the fear). We will return to the issue of impairment later in this chapter.

features of animal phobias

Animal phobias typically involve an experience of panic and fear upon confronting the feared animal, avoidance of the feared animal, anxious thinking patterns, and a feeling of disgust.

panic and fear

When people with phobias encounter a feared animal, their bodies react almost immediately to deal with the perceived danger. The reaction is often called a *fight-or-flight* reaction because the response is typically one of aggression (for example, immediately killing a spider) or, more typically, one of escape (running away from a bee). Many of the symptoms experienced during fear are physical, and the fear response is often referred to as a *panic attack*. A panic attack is simply an experience of fear that comes on quickly and is accompanied by at least four of the following symptoms: (1) racing or pounding heart, (2) sweating, (3) trembling or shaking, (4) shortness of breath, (5) feelings of choking, (6) chest pain or tightness, (7) nausea, (8) dizziness or lightheadedness, (9) feeling unreal or detached, (10) numbness or tingling sensations, (11) chills or hot flushes, (12) fear of dying, and (13) fear of going crazy or losing control. Most people with animal phobias experience panic attacks when they encounter their feared animals.

avoidance of the feared animal

In addition to the experience of panic, one of the most important features of animal phobias is the tendency to avoid the feared animal. In fact, the urge to escape from the feared animal can be overwhelming. People with animal phobias will often do whatever they can to avoid the feared animal, sometimes even putting themselves at risk. For example, we once worked with a woman who was fearful of spiders. One day she was backing out of her driveway when she saw a spider in her car. She was so terrified that she quickly opened the car door and exited the car—while it was still moving. Fortunately, a friend sitting in the passenger seat was able to stop the car and prevent an accident.

Other examples of avoidance include the following:

◊ Crossing the street after seeing a dog approaching on a leash

◊ Avoiding parks for fear of seeing a bird

◊ Avoiding swimming in lakes or oceans for fear of encountering fish

◊ Avoiding vacations in tropical climates for fear of seeing a large spider

◊ Avoiding watching nature shows on television for fear of seeing a snake

◊ Turning down an invitation to a picnic to avoid seeing bugs

Sometimes patterns of avoidance can be more extreme. For example, we have seen individuals who cannot even say the word "spider" or "snake." One person we worked with would not take baths because of her fear of fish. She knew that she was unlikely to see a fish in her own bathtub, but being in the tub still made her fearful because it reminded her of situations (like swimming in a lake) where she might see fish. Another individual would not even walk on the floor in her own living room for fear of encountering spiders. At bedtime, she would make her way from the living room sofa to the stairs by jumping from one piece of furniture to the next, with her feet never touching the floor.

Avoidance may also be more subtle. For example, people often do small things to protect themselves from feared animals. They may rely on *safety cues*—items they carry with them in order to feel safe. One person we know who is fearful of dogs always carries a box of dog biscuits with him when walking around his neighborhood. Upon seeing a dog, he throws a dog biscuit in one direction while he runs off in the other direction hoping that the dog will chase after the biscuit. In this example, the dog biscuits are a safety cue because they make him feel more comfortable while walking around. Of course, the very smart dogs—perhaps the ones who can read the package—see that he has a whole box of biscuits and they run after him instead of the biscuit he threw!

Other examples of subtle avoidance behaviors, overprotective behaviors, and reliance on safety cues include the following:

◊   Wearing long pants so spiders don't crawl
      on your legs

◊   Closing your eyes at a movie during a scene
      involving snakes

- ◊ Carrying pepper spray in case of encountering a dog

- ◊ Having a family member scope out the neighborhood before you leave the house, to make sure there are no cats around

- ◊ Carrying bug spray with you at all times

Avoidance, whether obvious or subtle, can lead to a number of problems. First, it is the avoidance that often leads to the most interference in your life. Second, by avoiding a feared animal, you never get to learn that the situation is actually safe. Learning to confront situations, rather than avoid them, is a key component of overcoming any phobia.

anxious thinking

People who fear animals often have anxious beliefs about their feared animals that are either untrue or exaggerated. For example, if you fear birds, you may assume that birds can tell when you are anxious and that allowing your anxiety to show increases the chances of a bird flying toward you. In fear, there is also a tendency for your attention to focus more narrowly on the source of the threat. For example, if you fear spiders, you may automatically scan each room you enter for signs of spiders. If there is a spider in the room, you may be the first person to find it. In fact, if there is a black dot on the wall, you may be the first person to find that (or anything else that reminds you of a spider) as well.

People who are fearful of animals also tend to perceive and remember information in a way that supports their fearful beliefs. They may remember a dog they saw previously as being larger than it really was. They may also ignore information that is inconsistent with their anxious beliefs (they may ignore all the dogs they encounter that are unaggressive). Fear is also associated with a tendency to interpret certain events as dangerous when, in fact, they are not. For example, someone who is fearful of snakes may misconstrue a snake's normal movements as a sign it is going to attack.

Not surprisingly, if you believe an animal is dangerous and if you only pay attention to and remember aspects of the situation that confirm your fear, you will continue to be afraid of the animal. An important step in overcoming an animal phobia is learning to think about the animal in a more balanced and realistic way. Exposing yourself to the animal you fear is one strategy for changing the way you think. Learning more about your feared animal, and directly examining whether the evidence supports your anxious beliefs, may also be helpful.

the role of disgust

Fear is not the only emotion that people with animal phobias report during encounters with a feared animal. A number of researchers have shown that a common experience shared by many people who fear spiders, snakes, rats, and certain other animals is a feeling of disgust (Woody and Teachman 2000). In other words, in addition to experiencing a sense of danger or threat in the situation, people may experience a sense of revulsion or being "grossed out." In fact, many of the challenges confronted by contestants on the television show *Fear Factor* are actually designed to trigger disgust. One contestant described the experience of having to eat worms during an appearance on the show in this way: "It was disgusting. I threw up. It was horrible." The emotions of fear and disgust may go hand in hand in some situations.

If your reaction to a feared animal tends to be one of disgust, there are a couple of things you should keep in mind as you work though this book. First, the treatments described in this book are effective, regardless of whether a person experiences high levels of disgust during exposure to the animal they fear (Merckelbach et al. 1993). Second, researchers have shown that treatment leads to decreases in disgust reactions in addition to decreases in fear (de Jong, Andrea, and Muris 1997).

who develops animal phobias?

Almost 6 percent of individuals suffer from a fear of animals that is severe enough to cause significant interference in their lives (Curtis et al. 1998). The prevalence of phobias regarding creepy, crawly animals (spiders, snakes, mice, and bugs) is considerably higher (6.63 percent of women and 2.44 percent of men) than that for other types of animals, such as dogs, cats, and birds (1.42 percent of women and 0.33 percent of men) (Bourdon et al. 1988).

You may notice from these statistics that 70 to 80 percent of people with animal phobias are women. Why would animal phobias be more common in women than in men? There are a number of possible explanations. First, one of the triggers for fear is watching other people behave fearfully. In Western cultures, women may have more role models for learning to fear animals than do men. For example, in movies and on television, it is much more common to see a female character showing fear of an animal (and perhaps a male character protecting her from the animal) than the other way around. Even in cartoons, it is common to see a woman (but never a man) standing on a chair screaming in terror when a mouse is in the room. Children learn to fear situations in part by watching others who are similar to them act fearfully.

Other cultural factors may also play a role. In many societies, it is more acceptable for women to express fear than it is for men to express fear. Men may therefore be more likely to confront feared situations rather than allow themselves to avoid situations and risk being ridiculed or suffer other negative consequences. In fact, there is even evidence that in comparison to women, men are more likely to downplay or underestimate their fears (Pierce and Kirkpatrick 1992). Finally, it is possible that there are biological differences between men and women that make women more vulnerable to developing animal phobias.

On average, animal phobias tend to begin at an earlier age, relative to other types of phobias. In fact, many people report having had their animal phobia for as long as they can recall. Whereas some studies have found an average age of onset for animal phobias in early childhood (for example, ages four or five), several other studies have found an average age of onset in the mid-teens (Antony and Barlow 2002). One reason for the different findings across studies is that many researchers fail to take into account the distinction between the onset of the fear itself, versus the onset of the full blown phobia. The average person experiences a fear of animals for several years before it reaches a level at which it causes interference in the person's life (Antony, Brown, and Barlow 1997).

the impact of phobias

Remember, a fear of animals becomes a true animal phobia when the fear is so strong that it impairs your functioning. People often trivialize phobias. They may think, "Who cares if you are afraid of dogs? Just don't get a dog." Though some animal fears can be trivial, true animal phobias are not. They can seriously interfere with your day-to-day life. Fortunately, they also respond very well to treatment. Below are some examples of how particular animal phobias can get in the way, either for an individual or for his or her family:

> ◊　Jacob's family had been planning a trip to the Grand Canyon for almost a year. They had to cancel the trip at the last minute

when Jacob read about the large spiders that live in Arizona.

◊ Amy was a thirty-five-year-old lawyer who moved from her own house into her parents' home after seeing two cockroaches in her living room. Even though her house had been fumigated and there were no signs of cockroaches anymore, she could not return to her home even two months after seeing the cockroaches.

◊ Janet refuses to visit her in-laws because they own a dog. Even if they lock the dog in one of the bedrooms, she still doesn't feel safe.

◊ Zachary is a teacher who left work for the day after one of his second grade students brought in a small snake for "show and tell."

◊ Parmjit will not leave her home if she sees a squirrel outside her window. On occasion, she is late for work, from waiting up to an hour for a squirrel to leave.

◊ During the summer months, Lauren cannot go anywhere where she might encounter birds. She avoids the beach, eating in outdoor cafés, walking in her neighborhood, and visiting parks. It affects what she and her family do on the weekends, and it even affects her job as a real estate agent. During the summer months, she typically has her clients explore the outdoor areas of houses that they are considering while she waits inside.

◊ On a typical night, it takes Roberta more than two hours to fall asleep. Before getting into bed, she checks throughout her room for spiders. She keeps the light on all night, so she can see a spider if one appears. She sleeps fully clothed to keep spiders off her body, and she often wakes up in the middle of night from a nightmare involving spiders.

overcoming animal phobias

Though animal phobias are among the most common phobias, they are also among the most treatable. In fact, many people with animal phobias can overcome their fears in just a few hours or days. There are numerous well-designed studies documenting effective treatments for phobias of snakes, spiders, and rats (Antony and Swinson 2000). There are also smaller studies and case reports on treating other types of animal phobias (including fear of birds, sharks, mice, dogs, cats, and others), suggesting that similar treatments work for a wide range of animal fears.

An essential component of effective treatment for any animal phobia is prolonged exposure to the animal. But don't worry—we don't expect you to spend hours with the animal you fear right away. The exposure occurs gradually. For example, you may start with looking at the animal from far away, looking at pictures of the animal, or even just saying the name of the animal. Even these limited forms of exposure will begin to erode your fear. As your fear decreases, you will be encouraged to move to the next steps, which involve increasing the intensity of the exposure. For example, this might involve moving a bit closer to the animal. Eventually, you will reach a point at which you can be close to the animal and even touch it with little fear (assuming it is not dangerous, like a venomous snake).

To be effective, exposure needs to be predictable. In other words, you should know what is going to happen and when it will happen. You should also know that you can terminate the exposure at any point if the need arises (although it is always best not to escape from the situation early). You will further increase the likelihood of success if you schedule your exposure practices close together, make sure that you stay in the situation until your fear comes down, and try to practice in a number of different locations and situations. You will learn to stop using subtle avoidance strategies such as distraction, overprotective behaviors, and safety cues. Such behaviors are thought to maintain your fear over time and may interfere with the benefits of exposure.

As you can imagine, exposure may be something that you cannot do on your own. For example, if you fear mice, you will probably not be able to buy a mouse at a pet store to use for your exposure practices. Finding a helper (a family member or friend who can practice exposures with you) may be essential. In some cases, treatment with a trained therapist may be the best option. This issue is discussed in more detail in chapter 4.

Learning to think differently about the animal may also be useful. Chapter 6 discusses detailed strategies for identifying your anxious beliefs and predictions, examining whether they are accurate, and learning to replace anxious thoughts with more realistic beliefs. These strategies are meant to be used in addition to exposure (not as a substitute for exposure).

A key to maintaining your gains after you have overcome your fear is to continue occasional exposures to the animal and to deal with any return of fear as it arises, before it gets out of hand. Chapter 7 discusses strategies for maintaining your improvement over the long term.

We recommend that any family members who are affected by your fear, as well as any individuals who will be helping you to overcome your fear, read this book, paying extra attention to the information in chapter 8.

Summary

This chapter offered an overview of the nature of animal phobias and their treatment. The most common animal phobias include fears of creepy, crawly animals, such as snakes, spiders, bugs, and mice. Phobias of dogs, cats, birds, and other animals are also common. Animal phobias tend to begin in childhood, and they occur more frequently in women than in men. People with animal phobias often experience a panic attack upon exposure to the animal. Panic and fear are accompanied by intense physical symptoms, such as a racing heart, shaking, breathlessness, and dizziness. Feelings of disgust are also common. You may have a strong desire to avoid the animal and to use behaviors designed to protect yourself from the feared animal. These fears often lead to a significant interference in your day-to-day life. Fortunately, treatment is effective and relatively brief. Exposure to feared animals is an essential component of treatment for animal phobias. Learning to change anxious patterns of thinking about animals may also be useful.

where do animal phobias come from?

Marc was a successful engineer who always prided himself on getting things done and doing them well. The one thing that Marc felt was holding him back in his life was a very severe fear of birds. Whenever he would see a bird, Marc would experience an extreme fear reaction that would take over his whole body. Although he knew his fear didn't make a lot of sense, it made it difficult for him to go anywhere there were birds. He avoided his backyard until he built a screened-in porch so he could be outside without allowing the birds to get close. He also avoided going down by the water, to parks, and to pet stores. Marc and his fiancée had planned a trip to Venice for their honeymoon. When Marc was researching for the trip, he learned that one of the most famous sites in Venice was a square that was filled with pigeons. Marc found that he was becoming anxious even thinking about the trip and about being around lots of birds. This is when he became motivated to overcome his fear.

When Marc came for treatment, one of his first questions was "Why did I get this fear?" Like a lot of people who develop a phobia, he wondered, "Why *me?*" It was hard for Marc to understand where the fear came from. "I am successful and confident in so many areas of my life. I know this fear doesn't make sense, but I can't control what happens to my body when I see a bird. It's like the fear just takes over." One of the first steps in helping Marc to overcome his fear was to help him understand how his fear may have developed and the factors that may have played a role for him.

pathways to developing fear

Often, people develop phobias through their learning experiences. Psychologist S. Rachman (1977) proposed three different learning pathways to developing fear: direct personal experience, observational experience, and informational or instructional experience. Over the years, researchers have shown that these pathways often contribute to the development of phobias. Each is described below.

direct personal experience

One pathway to developing an animal phobia involves having a negative experience with an animal. Being bitten or chased by a dog may lead to a phobia of dogs, for example. Or having an unexpected panic attack when a spider crawls on you may trigger a phobia of spiders. As these examples illustrate, the negative experience may involve being physically hurt or it may involve experiencing very intense fear and panic sensations while interacting with the animal or insect.

observational experience

Another way in which people may develop an animal phobia is by observing other people having a negative experience with the animal or by observing someone else behaving fearfully around the animal. If your grandmother is terrified of snakes and you observe her screaming each time she encounters a snake in the backyard, you may also develop a fear of snakes. Similarly, if you witness your friend being attacked by a dog, you may develop a fear of dogs.

informational or instructional experience

A phobia can also develop through information that you receive during the course of your life. Kathleen developed a bee phobia at quite a young age. Her father was allergic to bee stings. Kathleen recalled that when she was growing up, her family didn't eat any meals out in the backyard. They also made sure there were no flowers in the garden that might attract bees. Whenever Kathleen would go in and out of the house, she would be told to shut the door behind her to make sure that no bees would get into the house. It is not surprising that Kathleen developed an intense fear of bees, as one of the strong messages that she learned while growing up was that bees were dangerous and the likelihood of being stung was high.

People may also develop a phobia through information they read in a book or article, or through the media (from newspaper accounts, television, and movies). For example, many people with a phobia of sharks report that their fear began after seeing the movie *Jaws*. The mass media also plays a role in creating fear by the frequency with which they report stories on particular topics. For example, in the summer of 2001, the news media greatly increased public fears about sharks by dramatically increasing the frequency of reports on shark attacks. One popular news magazine ran a cover story entitled "The Summer of the Shark." This sort of headline contributed to the public perception that there was an increased risk of shark attacks that summer.

The National Marine Fisheries Service reported that the actual number of unprovoked shark attacks in the United States in 2001 was seventy-six compared to eighty-six the year before. So, in fact, the number of life-threatening shark attacks during the Summer of the Shark had not increased from the year before, but actually it was slightly lower. The media coverage also focused on the most serious attacks, where significant harm had occurred, despite the fact that most shark attacks are not life threatening. In fact, according to George Burgess, director of the University of Florida's International Shark Attack File and a noted shark researcher, ten times more people are killed by falling coconuts each year than are killed by shark attacks (UniSci International Science News 2002). This example shows how increased media coverage of shark attacks created the perception of greater danger and consequently raised the public's fears. In this way, the media sometimes helps to contribute to the development of phobias.

EXERCISE: Where Did Your Phobia Come From?

Thinking about your own fear, where do you think it originated? In your journal, record your responses to the following questions:

◊   Have you ever had a traumatic or negative experience with the animal? If so, describe what happened.

◊   Do you remember ever seeing someone have a negative experience with the animal (for example, being hurt or having extreme fear)? If so, describe what happened.

◊ Did you receive messages from your family when growing up that the animal was dangerous or something to be avoided? If so, describe the messages you received.

◊ Did your fear develop after reading or hearing frightening information about the animal in the media? If so, describe what you read or heard.

◊ Did your fear develop after having an extreme anxiety reaction to the animal? If so, describe what happened.

If you answered yes to one or more of these questions, then your phobia may have originated through your learning experiences. If you answered no to all of these questions, or if your fear has been present for as long as you can remember, you may simply be unaware of the experiences that contributed to your fear (they may have happened so long ago that you don't remember), or your fear may be related to factors other than these three pathways. Regardless of how your fear developed, the recommended treatment approach is the same, and you will likely be able to overcome your phobia by following the strategies described in this book.

other factors that affect fear development

A significant number of people with animal phobias report that they have "always" had the fear or that the fear has been present for as long as they can remember. Often, these people deny experiencing, observing, or hearing about a negative incident with the animal. To help explain this finding, Poulton and Menzies (2002) proposed a fourth pathway to developing fear that doesn't involve a specific history of learning. According to their theory, biological factors such as genetics may help to explain why some people develop fears and phobias in the absence of any negative experiences involving the feared situation. When Marc was being assessed for his bird phobia, he reported that his fear of birds had been present since he was very small. He denied ever having been hurt or experiencing a negative incident with a bird. He also indicated that nobody in his family really could understand where his fear came from because none of his family members were afraid of birds. It may be that Marc was genetically predisposed to develop an animal phobia. Of course, it may also be that he did have a negative experience but has no recollection of it.

Explaining the development of a phobia as occurring either as a result of learning or as a result of your biological makeup is probably an oversimplification. It is not unusual to find that with two people who are genetically identical (identical twins), one twin has a phobia and the other twin does not. So, biology doesn't explain everything. It is also not difficult to find two people who have both had a similar negative experience with an animal, but only one develops a fear of the animal. In fact, negative experiences that sometimes trigger phobias are equally common among individuals without phobias (Merckelbach et al. 1992). The percentage of people who have been bitten by a dog is similar among people with dog phobias and people without dog phobias. So learning experiences are not the whole story either.

Instead of trying to explain phobias as a result of either learning or biology, it probably makes more sense to explain them in terms of a complex interaction between someone's learning experiences and biological makeup. Only then can you begin to appreciate why some people develop phobias following a negative experience and others don't.

There are a number of other factors that may help influence who develops a phobia following a negative experience. These are discussed below.

preparedness

One interesting fact about phobias is that they tend to develop for certain stimuli and not others. Seligman (1971) proposed the idea that we are predisposed or "prepared" to learn certain associations that lead to fear. For example, we may be more likely to fear snakes after being bitten by one than to fear plants after being pricked by a cactus. Seligman proposed that we developed this preparedness to fear certain things as a means of ensuring our survival. When you think about it, it makes sense that we would be more likely to develop fear toward animals that could potentially be dangerous (a snake) than to more benign animals (a butterfly).

In support of this theory, snake phobias are more common then butterfly phobias. However, there are people who have developed phobias of animals and insects that do not seem inherently dangerous, such as pigeons, ladybugs, even butterflies. In fact, we recently treated an individual with a phobia of butterflies. So preparedness theory explains the development of some phobias better than others.

genetic factors

The finding that specific phobias tend to run in families suggests that genetics may play a role in the development of a specific phobia, though learning may also affect the transmission of phobias from generation to generation. Studies that have attempted to tease apart the effects of genetics and environment have suggested that genetics increases the likelihood of developing an animal phobia by as much as 47 percent (Kendler, Karkowski, and Prescott 1999). For example, if you have a first-degree relative (a parent, brother, or sister) with an animal phobia, you are at a greater risk for developing an animal phobia, and genetics plays a part in that increased risk.

One study found that individuals who have a close relative with a specific phobia had a higher rate of having a specific phobia (31 percent) than did individuals without a similar family history (11 percent) (Fyer et al. 1990). Although having a relative with a specific phobia may increase your risk for developing a specific phobia, the phobia that people develop is usually different from that in the relative, although it is often from the same general type. For example, both you and your dad may have an animal phobia but you may fear fish and he may fear snakes.

disgust sensitivity

There is some evidence that a tendency to experience disgust in response to certain stimuli may be important in the development of some animal phobias (Davey, Forster, and Mayhew 1993). For example, whenever Lisa would see a mouse, she described feeling "disgusted" by it. She thought it was dirty and repulsive. She also felt a lot of fear whenever she would see or hear about rodents. Lisa's tendency to feel disgusted by rodents may have played a role in the development of her mouse phobia. Lisa did not report feeling disgusted by other animals or insects, and she did not have any other phobias.

personality factors

Certain aspects of your personality may also make it more likely for you to have developed an animal phobia. For example, your general level of anxiousness (sometimes called "trait anxiety") can play a role. Researchers believe that anxiety-prone people are more likely to develop a phobia than those who are not generally anxious. Your beliefs about how much you can control a situation may also have an effect on whether you develop a phobia. If you have a high degree of perceived control over a situation, you are less likely to develop a phobia than if you have less perceived control. Note that it is your perception of control that affects whether phobias are likely to develop—not whether you actually have control.

previous exposure to the animal

Previous exposure to an animal may protect you from developing an animal phobia. For example, if you grew up with dogs, you may be less likely to develop a dog phobia after being bitten by one than you would be if you never had a dog.

subsequent exposure to the animal

What happens after a negative experience is also important. You have probably heard the expression "If you fall off a horse, you should get back on as quickly as possible." If you are exposed to the animal after a negative experience, you may be less likely to develop a phobia than you would be without continued exposure. In other words, someone who is exposed to dogs after being bitten by one will be less likely to develop a fear of dogs.

Someone who avoids being around dogs after being bitten will be more likely to develop a phobia.

Once a phobia develops, it is not likely to go away on its own. Treatment is often necessary to overcome a phobia because one of the things that people do when they have a severe fear is avoid the feared animal. Avoidance is a major factor in maintaining your fear because it prevents you from having the opportunity to experience your fear decrease in the presence of the feared animal. When you avoid the animal, you are prevented from having new learning experiences that help to eliminate your fear. As you will see in the next few chapters, one of the most critical strategies for overcoming your phobia is gradual exposure to the feared animal or insect. This may seem scary to you at this point, but remember, you will be proceeding at a pace that works for you.

other factors

Stress at work or in a relationship at the time of a negative experience around an animal may also play a role in phobia development by making you more likely to react fearfully. In addition, the context of the event may influence your reaction. Being bitten by a dog when you have a supportive person with you may protect you from developing fear, as opposed to being bitten when you are alone.

Summary

This chapter discussed the different types of negative learning experiences that can lead to the development of an animal phobia, including learning through direct personal experience, through observing someone having a negative experience, and through information received from family members or the media. Some people develop an animal phobia without a direct or indirect learning experience. Many factors may increase the likelihood that someone develops a phobia. These factors include preparedness, genetics, disgust sensitivity, personality characteristics, experience before and after a negative event, the context of a negative event, and stress. Understanding how your phobia may have developed can help as you prepare to tackle your fear.

3

developing a hierarchy

Now that you have a better sense of where your animal phobia comes from, you are ready for the next step in tackling your fear. A major component of treatment for your animal phobia is gradual exposure to your fears. Before you get to exposure, however, you need to identify the situations you avoid because of your fear and the different factors that influence the intensity of your fear in these situations. You will then use this information to develop an exposure hierarchy.

what is a hierarchy?

An exposure hierarchy is a list of situations that you would typically avoid because of your phobia. This list is specific to your fear and based on your own personal experiences. The items are ranked from the most fear-provoking situation to the least fear-provoking situation. The hierarchy is an important tool for helping to guide the exposure practices that are described beginning in chapter 5. Ideally, it should consist of ten to fifteen items that provide a good sampling of the situations you fear and avoid. The sample hierarchy below was developed by Jenny, a thirty-year-old woman with a snake phobia. Note how she formulated her list as a series of actions.

Example: Jenny's Exposure Hierarchy		
Item	Description	Fear Rating (0–100)
1	Hold a live black snake, about three feet long.	100
2	Touch a live black snake (about three feet long) that someone else is holding.	100
3	Stand three feet away from someone else who is holding a live black snake, about three feet long.	98
4	Stand six feet away from someone else who is holding a live black snake, about three feet long.	95
5	Visit a reptile store and look at the snakes.	95

6	Take a walk in the woods.	90
7	Watch a video of snakes, of various colors and sizes.	90
8	Hold a large, green rubber snake.	85
9	Look at a large, green rubber snake.	80
10	Work in the garden.	75
11	Look at a color picture of a snake.	70
12	Touch a black-and-white picture of a snake.	65
13	Look at a black-and-white picture of a snake with its head uncovered.	60
14	Look at a black-and-white picture of a snake with its head covered.	55
15	Say the word "snake."	50

As you can see, there are fifteen situations in Jenny's hierarchy. Although Jenny probably avoids or feels frightened in more than fifteen situations, what she chose to list provides a good representation of the situations that are most difficult for her. As you construct your own hierarchy, you do not need to include every single situation that is a problem for you. Rather, you should select ten to fifteen items that best capture the types of situations that are problematic for you. You should also try to be as specific as possible. For example, if you are more afraid of larger dogs than smaller dogs, be sure to specify the size of the dog in your description. (We will return to this issue and how to develop your own hierarchy later in this chapter.)

Also notice that Jenny's fear ratings on her hierarchy range from the least anxiety-provoking situation of saying the word "snake" (fear rating of 50) to the most anxiety-provoking situation of holding a live snake (fear rating of 100). It is helpful to rate your fear on a scale of 0 to 100, so you can order the situations you have identified in terms of the intensity of the fear that each one triggers. To help you determine fear ratings, it is useful to establish your anchor points. Think about the most fear-provoking experience that you have had with your animal phobia. It may have been a time when your fear was so intense you thought it would overwhelm you. This level of fear would represent a rating of 100 for you. Now, think about a time when you felt no fear at all and you were completely comfortable. This level of fear would represent a rating of 0 for you. Once you have an idea of what 0 and 100 mean for you, it should be easier for you to rate situations in between. A 50 would represent a moderate level of fear. People often initially find it difficult to rate their fear. Usually, doing so becomes easier with practice.

Below are some more samples of exposure hierarchies for various phobias.

Example: Hierarchy for Sam's Dog Phobia		
Item	Description	Fear Rating (0–100)
1	Touch the face of a golden retriever or other large dog.	100
2	Touch the back of a golden retriever or other large dog.	99
3	Stand one foot from a large dog on a leash.	95
4	Stand five feet from a large dog on a leash.	90
5	Stand ten feet from a large dog on a leash.	85
6	Sit on a park bench and look at dogs on leashes.	80
7	Walk by a large dog without crossing the street.	80
8	Hold a puppy or small dog.	75
9	Touch a puppy or small dog.	70
10	Stand one foot from a puppy or small dog on a leash.	65
11	Stand five feet from a puppy or small dog on a leash.	60

12	Stand ten feet from a puppy or small dog on a leash.	55
13	Watch a video clip of various dogs.	50
14	Touch pictures of various dogs.	40
15	Look at pictures of various dogs.	30

Example: Hierarchy for Leslie's Spider Phobia		
Item	Description	Fear Rating (0–100)
1	Hold a harmless, medium-sized spider in my hand.	100
2	Touch a spider web.	95
3	Touch a harmless, medium-sized spider.	95
4	Put hand in plastic bin containing a medium-sized spider (without actually touching the spider).	90
5	Hold sealed jar with a medium-sized spider in it.	85
6	Stand beside a sealed jar containing a medium-sized spider.	80
7	Stand five feet from a sealed jar containing a medium-sized spider.	75

8	Walk around the basement.	70
9	Touch a large plastic spider.	60
10	Look at a large plastic spider.	55
11	Touch a color picture of a large spider.	50
12	Look at a color picture of a large spider.	45
13	Touch a cartoon drawing of a small spider.	40
14	Look at a cartoon drawing of a small spider.	40
15	Say the word "spider."	35

developing a list of feared situations

The first step in developing your own hierarchy is to construct a list of the situations that you fear or avoid because of your animal phobia. When Jenny was constructing her hierarchy, she could never have imagined actually holding a live snake, but she included this situation on her list because she knew that if she could do that she would have really conquered her fear. When you are constructing your hierarchy, don't just limit yourself to situations that you think you can do. Be sure to include situations that you may not be able to do now but that you would really like to be able to do if you didn't have a phobia (holding a cat, patting a dog, playing with a harmless spider on its web, feeding a pigeon, touching a fish). Think about your hierarchy as a wish list. If you didn't have your phobia, what sorts of things would you be doing differently?

EXERCISE:
List Your Feared Situations

In your journal, make a list of the situations that you avoid or fear because of your phobia. Be sure to include situations in which you would like to feel comfortable. Be as specific as possible. For now, don't worry about putting the situations in any order or rating them.

identifying factors that influence your fear

One thing that you may notice in Jenny's hierarchy was that looking at the face of the snake was more anxiety provoking than looking at the snake's body. This was one factor that influenced Jenny's fear. Other factors included whether the snake was moving or not, the color and size of the snake, whether the tongue was sticking out, and the position it was in (moving or curled up with its head raised). Other relevant variables were whether she was touching or looking at the snake, how close she was to it, and whether the snake was in a picture or video, was a rubber snake, or was live. Each of these factors influenced the level of fear Jenny experienced, and many of these factors were incorporated in her exposure hierarchy. By incorporating factors that influence your fear, you can generate situations that are more or less fear provoking for you. Ideally, your fear ratings should range from about 30 or 40 in intensity to 100. If you find that all of your items are rated very high, it may be difficult to start tackling the situations. By incorporating greater or fewer of the factors that influence your fear, you can increase or decrease the range in fear intensity.

Below are common factors that may influence your fear (with examples in parentheses)

- ◇ Authenticity (a live bird vs. a stuffed toy bird, video, or photo)

- ◇ Size (a large dog vs. a small dog)

- ◇ Color (a brown snake vs. a red, yellow, or orange snake)

- ◇ Movement (a bird standing still or flying)

- ◇ Location (seeing a spider in your house vs. outside)

- ◇ Whether you are alone or with someone else

◊   Position of the animal (a snake lying straight out vs. curled with its head raised)

◊   Number (one pigeon vs. a group of pigeons)

◊   Noise (a dog barking or a cat hissing)

◊   Appearance (a snake with its tongue hidden vs. sticking out)

◊   Activity (a dog sitting quietly vs. tugging on a rope)

◊   Restraint or Control (a spider in a jar vs. running loose)

EXERCISE: List the Factors That Influence Your Fear

What are the factors that influence your fear? In your journal, record a list of variables that tend to affect the intensity of your fear and discomfort concerning the animal you fear.

---

generating your hierarchy

The next step is to generate your hierarchy by combining the situations that you listed above with the factors that you identified as influencing your fear. When your hierarchy is complete, you will be ready for the next steps in preparing for active treatment.

EXERCISE: Generate an Exposure Hierarchy

In your journal, develop an exposure hierarchy using the same format as the examples provided earlier in this chapter. As you generate items for your hierarchy, take into account the list of situations you recorded earlier as well as the factors that influence your fear. Include about ten to fifteen items in descending order (with the scariest items at the top). Once you have listed a number of items, beside each item rate your fear level from 0 to 100 based on how you would feel if you had to confront that situation *right now*.

Summary

In this chapter, the hierarchy was introduced as an important tool for guiding later exposure treatment. The steps in generating a hierarchy include listing situations that you fear or avoid, identifying factors that influence your fear, rating your exposure hierarchy items, and organizing your hierarchy items in descending order, based on your fear ratings.

4

preparing for treatment

Preparing for treatment involves these steps: identifying a helper to assist you in your treatment, finding the materials you will need to practice exposures on your hierarchy, and considering whether you want to seek professional help.

finding a helper

We highly recommend having a helper assist you in overcoming your phobia. Why do you need a helper? The helper plays an important role in the following ways:

⬥   Providing support

⬥   Gathering materials needed for exposure practices

⬥   Helping to set up exposure practices

⬥   Assisting during exposure practices

⬥   Demonstrating or modeling nonfearful coping behavior during exposure practices with the feared animal

Ideally, your helper should be a person with whom you have a trusting and close relationship (this could be your spouse, a friend, or a family member). Before getting started, your helper will need to be educated with respect to what his or her role will be. Reading chapter 8 on how to help someone with an animal phobia is a good place to start, though he or she would benefit from reading this entire book. Keep a number of characteristics in mind when selecting your helper. First, choose someone who is familiar with your fear and with whom you are willing to allow your fear to show. This person should be someone who is patient, supportive, understanding, and kind, and not someone who is pushy, impatient, or who is likely to trivialize your fear or to become angry or frustrated if you get frightened or decide to escape from the situation. Be sure to choose someone who has no fear of the animal. He or she should be willing to devote the time needed to read the relevant chapters in this book, to help you gather the materials you need, and to work with you during your exposure practices.

To illustrate the role that a helper might play in your treatment, consider the following example. Sam had developed a phobia of dogs after being attacked when he was seven years old. When he was twenty-eight, just after getting married, he decided it was time to overcome his fear of dogs. Sam had two reasons for wanting to tackle his phobia. First, his wife, who grew up around dogs, really wanted to get one. Second, and more importantly for Sam, he wanted to make sure that his children never developed a phobia like his. Sam wanted to be comfortable around dogs so that his children wouldn't be influenced by his fear. Sam's exposure hierarchy was shown in chapter 3.

Sam's wife volunteered to be his helper. Not only did she provide support, but she also played an important role in helping Sam tackle situations on his hierarchy that would be difficult for him to do on his own. For example, when Sam was ready, his wife held the neighbor's friendly, eight-year-old poodle on her lap as Sam slowly approached from a distance of thirty feet. As Sam found his fear decreasing, he would take another step toward his wife and the dog. With each step closer, his fear would increase temporarily; he would remain in that position until it decreased again and he felt ready to move closer. After two hours, Sam was able to stand beside the dog with relatively little fear or discomfort. On another day, Sam's wife held the dog while Sam worked on touching it. First, his wife stroked the dog's back, and then Sam touched the dog in the same way. They repeated this step until Sam's fear level was below 30 on a 0 to 100 point scale. Then they moved to the next step, working toward the goal of patting the dog's head, which was the most fear-provoking situation for Sam. In this way, Sam's wife modeled nonfearful coping behavior, which helped Sam to feel more comfortable and also taught him how to approach the situation.

If you are unable to identify someone in your life who would be a good helper, either because there isn't anyone or because you prefer to keep things private, you have a couple of options. You can try to proceed on your own, without a helper. If you encounter difficulties, then getting professional help would be the next step. Or you can seek a professional helper straight away. We will talk about where to find professional help at the end of this chapter.

Regardless of whether you decide to proceed with a helper, the next step in treatment is finding the items that you will need for your exposure practices.

finding materials for exposure practice

The hierarchy that you developed in chapter 3 provides a guide to the materials you will need to have on hand as you do your exposure practices. For example, looking at Jenny's hierarchy from chapter 3, you can see that she will need the following items to complete treatment: pictures of snakes in black-and-white and in color, rubber snakes, a video clip of snakes, a reptile store, and a live black snake. Below is a list of places where Jenny could find these items.

Item	Where to Find It
pictures of snakes—black-and-white, color	books or magazines from the library, bookstore, children's bookstore, hobby shop, nature shop, Internet search, snake calendar
rubber snake	toy store, museum, hobby store, nature shop
video with snakes in it	video rental store, online video and DVD store, the library, a friend's video of snakes in a pet store or reptile store, a television show featuring snakes
live snake	Ask the owner of a pet or reptile store if you can borrow or rent a snake for the weekend. Have your helper pick it up. If this isn't possible, consider practicing in the pet store. Or contact a zoo or tourist attraction (such as Reptile World) to see if someone would be willing to assist with exposures.

As you might imagine, because of her phobia, Jenny would have a hard time getting all of these things on her own. Here is where you can benefit from the help of someone who will be willing to get the materials you need and help you carry out your exposures. You don't need to have all your materials up front. Rather, as you work through the steps in your hierarchy, you can get the materials you need to reach each relevant step. It is normal to feel some anxiety as you are preparing for treatment. Keep in mind that you will be working at your own pace in a gradual manner.

We have listed below some of the common materials you might need for different phobias, as well as ideas of where to get them. Don't worry if your feared animal isn't specifically included below. Because animal phobias can occur for *any* animal, we limited our examples to the more common ones. The suggestions below would also apply to gathering materials related to other animals, such as butterflies, horses, bees, lizards, and so forth.

pictures

Pictures can be found in books from the library, a bookstore or children's bookstore, and in hobby or nature shops. If looking at a color photo is too difficult, you can begin with a black-and-white photo (for example, a photocopy of a color photo). Calendars are also a good source for pictures. If you have access to the Internet, there are many great Web sites with a wide variety of pictures. Some useful sites are listed in the table below.

Pictures	Web site
assorted animal pictures (insects, reptiles, dogs, cats, fish, birds, frogs, and so on)	http://www.thepetprofessor.com/secFree Photos/welcome.asp http://www.nationalgeographic.com/site index/animals.html
snakes	http://www.herp=pix.org/ http://www.pitt.edu/~mcs2/herp/SoNA. html http://simonsnakesite.tripod.com/
dogs	http://www.animaltime.net/dogs/dog_pic tures.html
cats	http://cats.about.com/od/catpictures/ http://www.fanciers.com/homepages.html
birds	http://www.stanford.edu/~petelat1/ http://www.naturesound.com/birds/birds. html http://www.birdpictures.net/
spiders	http://www.xs4all.nl/~ednieuw/Spiders/ ArgiopesUS/Argiopes_USA.html http://entomology.unl.edu/images/spiders /spiders.htm
mice	http://www.unusualposters.com/mice. htm
fish	http://marinefisheries.org/photo.htm

animal models and toys

Rubber animals or replicas can be found in hobby, craft, and nature shops. Toy stores and museums are also good sources. You can order animal models online (for example, at http://naturepavilion.com).

videos

Video clips of the animal that you fear may be found in the library, a video store, or online (try http://nature pavilion.com or http://shop.nationalgeographic.com). Your helper can make a video of the animal you fear either in the neighborhood or at a pet store or zoo. Another good source is television. There are a number of different channels devoted to animal shows (such as the cable channel *Animal Planet*). You can check your television listings for shows featuring the animal that you fear and then record the show on videotape to use when you are ready. Alternatively, you can have your helper do this for you.

Although animals depicted in documentaries and nature shows are often better for exposure practices, you can also use segments of popular movies that contain images of the animal that you fear. Keep in mind that in many cases the animal may be portrayed in a scary way. For example, in *Raiders of the Lost Ark*, Harrison Ford's character is confronted with a pit of snakes. Although your hierarchy may include watching scary videos involving your feared animal, it is often more useful to watch animals depicted in more realistic and less scary ways, particularly early in treatment. In addition, movies often show the animal for a very short amount of time. To do a practice properly, you may have to watch the sequence and rewind it repeatedly during exposure. A Web site that lists some movies that contain animals is http://happyand healthypets.com/nov22-03-animals-movies. html.

Some examples of popular movies that feature animals are listed below.

Animal	Movie
snakes	*Raiders of the Lost Ark*
spiders	*Spiderman* *Charlotte's Web*
insects	*Metamorphosis* *Patch Adams (butterfly)* *Joe's Apartment (cockroaches)*
birds	*The Birds* *The Crow* *Paulie* *Spirit of the Eagle*
dogs	*Old Yeller* *Benji* *Lassie* *101 Dalmatians* *Best in Show* *Turner and Hootch*

cats	The Adventures of Milo and Otis
	Men in Black
	Homeward Bound
	Fifth Element
mice and rats	The Green Mile
	Mouse Hunt
	Indiana Jones and the Last Crusade
	Stuart Little
	Dr. Dolittle
fish	The Perfect Storm
	Big Fish
	A Fish Called Wanda

live animals

You can borrow live animals from friends and family or view them in the wild or at a pet store, zoo, farm, or other location. You also can have your helper negotiate an arrangement for you to borrow or rent the animal that you need from a pet store. Or you can try getting permission to stay in a pet store for an hour or two after closing (by offering to pay the clerk or manager for his or her time) to work with birds or snakes. Below is a list of where you might obtain particular types of animals.

Birds. Pet stores are often a good source for birds. Ask the owner or manager of the pet store whether you can spend some time practicing exposure. In pet stores, you can practice with small birds in cages, as well as with larger birds that may not be in cages, such as parrots. You can also ask friends, colleagues, or family members who own pet birds to let you visit and spend time with their pets. For birds in the wild, a good source would be public parks, beaches, or squares. Though some birds (for example, sparrows) will fly away when you get close, others (such as pigeons) will often stick around, particularly if you feed them (an activity that may be near the top of your exposure hierarchy).

Dogs and cats. Public parks and sidewalks are a good place to find people walking their dogs on a leash. For a higher-level exposure practice, you can visit a local dog park or leashless park where dogs roam free. You can also get exposure to dogs and cats by visiting pet stores, the Humane Society, or friends and family members who have these pets.

Spiders and insects. Spiders and insects can often be found in basements, attics, gardens, wooded areas, and other locations. If you decide to collect spiders outdoors, be sure to use only harmless spiders (we often use a field guide to identify spiders before using them for exposure). Of course, if you live in an area where there are no poisonous spiders, this won't be an issue for you. University or college biology departments are another good source for spiders and insects. For example, at our local university, there is a researcher who studies cockroaches, and he has been very generous in supplying us with bugs over the years. We have also obtained spiders from some of the indoor pavilions at the local zoo. There are even companies that will send you spiders by courier. For example, the Carolina Biological Supply Company (www.caro lina.com) sells spiders and other animals for research and education. We have purchased harmless spiders from this company in the past. Check the Internet for other sources. Some insects (for example, crickets) can be purchased at pet stores. To attract moths, keep a light on outside. Bees can be found outdoors or may be obtained from beekeepers (we don't recommend trying to catch bees in the wild, though having lunch at an outdoor café with bees in the vicinity is perfectly appropriate).

Mice, rats, and snakes. Sources for these animals include pet stores, people who own these pets, and perhaps researchers in university biology or psychology departments. We recommend against handling mice, rats, and snakes caught in the wild, due to the possibility of contracting a disease or of being bitten.

Fish. You can go to a local pond, harbor, lake, or river to practice exposure to fish in a natural setting. For a practice nearer the top of your hierarchy, you can actually wade in and stand in the area where the fish are. Pet stores and aquariums are also good places to find fish. Seafood restaurants and grocery stores sell fish and sometimes display them live in an aquarium.

EXERCISE: What Materials Do You Need?

Using your hierarchy as a guide, as well as the suggestions provided earlier, make a list in your journal of items you will need and where you might find them. Before you begin the exposure practices described in chapter 5, you will need to gather the required materials, decide upon locations for your practices, and locate the animals you need. In all likelihood, these steps will be very anxiety provoking at first, and you will need to engage your helper to complete some of these tasks for you.

be prepared to feel anxious

It is very normal to feel anxiety as you prepare to tackle your fear. You probably experienced some anxiety just reading through this material on preparing for exposures. You may have had the thought, "Yeah, right. There is no way that I am going to be touching the animal that I fear!" This is a natural reaction. In fact, part of overcoming your fear will involve feeling some fear. Unfortunately, there is no way around this. We will try to make things easier by proceeding in a very gradual, stepwise manner so that you are always in control. When you do start practicing exposure, you may feel increased anxiety, irritability, stress, tearfulness, tension, headaches, and difficulty sleeping. These reactions are to be expected and are a part of the recovery process for some people. To cope with these feelings, it is helpful to plan time after exposures for you to relax and unwind (by taking a bath, going for a walk, reading a book, going for a run, or doing whatever feels good to you). We also recommend rewarding yourself every time you reach a new step on your hierarchy (doing something you enjoy, buying yourself a new book or CD, going out for dinner, and so on). It is helpful to keep an open mind as you work through the steps involved in overcoming your fear. You will be surprised at the outcome!

when to seek professional help

If you find it difficult to proceed on your own or with your helper—if you feel overwhelmed or too anxious to begin practicing items on your exposure hierarchy—it would be a good idea to seek professional help to assist you in overcoming your fear. You will want to identify a professional who is trained in treating anxiety disorders and specifically animal phobias. Make sure the therapist is familiar with the type of treatment described in this book, which is often called exposure therapy, behavior therapy, or cognitive behavioral therapy (CBT). It is very important that you feel comfortable with the therapist you choose. If you are unsure, it is better to keep interviewing until you find a good match. Some good resources include the following:

⋄   The Anxiety Disorders Association of America (ADAA), which may be accessed online at www.adaa.org or by phone at (240) 485-1001. The ADAA maintains a list of professionals throughout North America who are experienced in treating phobias, and it should have contact information for professionals in your community. The ADAA can also put you in touch with similar associations around the world, such as the Anxiety Disorders Association of Canada (www.anxietycanada.ca).

◊   Professional associations such as the Association for Advancement of Behavior Therapy (www.aabt.org) often provide referrals.

◊   A health care provider, such as your family physician or a therapist you are seeing for some other problem, may be able to provide you with the names of professionals or a referral to specialized anxiety services in your area.

Once you have identified a professional, you will want to gather information to determine whether he or she is suitable for your needs. You can use the questions below as a guide to gather information before making an appointment. We have indicated our recommendation after each question.

1.   *What is your professional training and background (e.g., psychiatrist, psychologist, clinical social worker, master's level therapist)?*
     Make sure that the person has some professional training in mental health

through an advanced degree, accreditation, or credentials.

2. *Do you have experience treating anxiety disorders?*
    Make sure that the person is experienced in treating anxiety disorders.

3. *Where did you do your anxiety disorder training?*
    Make sure that the person has received specific training in the treatment of anxiety disorders (ideally, experience at a specialized anxiety clinic or through an academic program).

4. *What type of treatment approach do you use? Are you experienced in cognitive behavioral therapy?*
    Make sure that the person practices behavior therapy or cognitive behavioral therapy. Be wary of professionals who recommend other approaches to therapy or who recommend a blend of different therapy approaches. Although a variety of treatments can be effective for overcoming problems with anxiety, depression, and other issues, exposure therapy (a type of behavior therapy) is the only type of treatment that has been proven to work for animal phobias.

5. *How many cases of animal phobia have you treated?*

Try to find a therapist who has had experience treating animal phobias and preferably the type of phobia that you have. If this is not possible, the skills and experience needed to administer exposure therapy for other types of phobias and anxiety problems (such as height phobias, obsessive-compulsive disorder, or agoraphobia) can often be applied successfully to the treatment of an animal phobia.

Summary

This chapter discussed the role that a helper may play in the recovery process and how to identify a helper. It reviewed how to prepare for exposure practices by identifying the materials you need and where to find them. Part of preparing for exposure therapy involves preparing to feel anxious and uncomfortable. In some cases, it may be necessary to seek professional help in order to overcome a phobia; this chapter also reviewed some strategies for finding an appropriate therapist.

confronting your fear

If there is one chapter from this book that you should read several times, it's this one. The only type of treatment that has been proven to be effective for the treatment of animal phobias is exposure to the feared animal. In fact, many people with phobias of spiders, bugs, snakes, dogs, cats, birds, and other animals can overcome their fear with only a few hours of intensive exposure (Antony and Barlow 2002).

In chapter 3 you identified a list of situations that you fear, as well as the factors that influence your fear in these situations. You developed a hierarchy, or a list of feared situations organized from most scary (at the top of the list) to least scary (at the bottom). Next, in chapter 4, you took a number of steps to prepare for treatment. You identified someone who can help out as you confront your feared animal and you planned steps to locate your feared animal in various forms (including pictures, models and toys, videos, and live animals).

Now, you are ready to start the process of overcoming your fear. This chapter describes in detail how to overcome your fear and reduce your avoidance using standard exposure-based techniques.

why avoidance is a problem

Some situations are difficult to avoid without leading to significant impairment in day-to-day functioning. For example, if you can't sit in your backyard or go into certain rooms in your home for fear of seeing a spider, you will be limited with respect to the types of things you can do. The more limited your activities are, the more likely your avoidance is to interfere with your job, school, relationships, family life, hobbies, recreation, and with your general enjoyment of life.

Also, although avoidance helps to reduce your fear in the short term (that's why you avoid the animal, after all), it tends to prevent your recovery from fear over the long term. Whenever you escape from your feared animal, you reinforce your fear. The acts of avoiding and escaping provide a sense of relief from fear, which in itself can feel very rewarding, making you more likely to do it again the next time you have an opportunity to come into contact with the animal. Avoidance also prevents you from ever learning that your fears are unfounded, or at least exaggerated. Avoiding a feared animal will make encounters with the animal even scarier later. Over the long term, the best way to fight your fear is to begin confronting it.

Remember, avoidance can take on more subtle forms as well. Chapter 1 listed some examples of subtle avoidance strategies and other safety behaviors that are designed to protect you in the feared situation (such as carrying pepper spray just in case a dog is encountered). These overprotective strategies have the same effect as avoidance. They reduce fear in the short term, but they also may strengthen your belief that the animal is dangerous, thereby making it more difficult to overcome the problem in the long term. Exposure strategies directly target the obvious and subtler forms of avoidance.

what to expect during exposure therapy

We are aware of no proven treatments for animal phobias that don't include some form of exposure. Therefore, a decision to successfully overcome your fear will need to include a willingness to tolerate some degree of discomfort along the way. As you begin to practice exposure, remember that you are in control of every step in the process. You are in charge of when you do the exposure, where you do it, what you are exposed to, how quickly you take steps, and when the exposure ends. In fact, exposure works best when you have a sense of control in the situation. It is important that nobody forces you to do anything that you haven't agreed to do (make sure your helper is aware of this requirement). Because you will be in control, the exposure will only be as difficult as you allow it to be. For example, you can adjust the intensity of the exposure by controlling how close you are to the animal.

Starting a program of exposure is like starting a new exercise regimen—it may take a while before you start to see the full benefits. At first, exposure may be frightening and exhausting. You may also notice an initial increase in anxiety, irritability, and a general "stressed out" feeling. You may also become more vigilant about your feared animal. For example, after you start exposing yourself to snakes, you may start to "see" snakes even when they aren't there (a stick on the ground may at first look like a snake). You may even have bad dreams about your feared animal. However, if you stick with your exposure practices, you will start to notice a reduction in fear. You will also see an improvement in the other negative feelings associated with starting a new exposure program. Sticking it out despite the initial discomfort will be well worth it. The discomfort you experience at the start will pass. Think of exposure as short-term pain (discomfort) for long-term gain (getting your life back).

getting the most out of exposure

Are you skeptical about whether exposure can work for you? Have you found in the past that exposures to your feared animal typically don't lead to a decrease in your fear? Or, even more concerning, have you had experiences with exposure that have made your fear worse? This experience is not unusual. The types of exposure you encounter on a day-to-day basis are unlikely to lead to a reduction in fear. The times that you encounter your feared animal in everyday life are probably unexpected, out of your control, too brief, and too infrequent to have any positive impact. In fact, unpredictable exposure may even lead to an increase in fear. This chapter highlights the most important features of exposure to keep in mind as you confront your fear. The suggestions given here are based on numerous studies showing how exposure should be conducted (Antony and Barlow 2002).

take steps at a pace that works for you

Exposure will probably work regardless of whether you take steps quickly or slowly. Each approach has advantages and disadvantages. The advantage of taking steps more slowly is that you will be likely to experience less discomfort and fear along the way. However, the smaller the steps you take, and the more slowly you work through your hierarchy, the longer it will take you to overcome your fear. There is nothing wrong with taking steps more quickly or with trying things that are higher up on your hierarchy if you want to. The worst thing that will happen is that your fear will be intense and that you will need to try something a bit easier the next time. The advantage of moving through your hierarchy items more quickly is that you will overcome the problem sooner. Seeing large improvements quickly can be very rewarding.

Ultimately, how quickly to take things is up to you. We recommend that you move through your hierarchy as quickly as you are willing to. In therapy settings, it is not unusual for people to be handling their feared animal comfortably after only a few sessions. If you are working on this without the benefit of a therapist, it may take longer. The key is to keep trying increasingly difficult items until they are no longer a problem.

When deciding where to start, it is useful to begin with an item that is likely to be challenging but not overwhelming. You don't have to start with the bottom item on your hierarchy if you think you can start with a higher item. For example, if you are willing to begin your exposures to birds by being near a live caged bird, there is no need to bother with easier items, like looking at photos of birds. The bottom line is that you should start as high on your hierarchy as you can, and you should move through items at a pace that is challenging but manageable.

plan practices in advance

We recommend that you plan your practices in advance, rather than just waiting until you feel comfortable or until the time is convenient. Exposure practices are rarely convenient and are almost never comfortable. It is useful to schedule your exposures in your date book, the way you would any other appointment. Otherwise, it will be very easy to put off practicing. Make sure your helper is available for the scheduled practices, especially early in the treatment, when you may need help setting up the exposure.

minimize surprises

One of the factors that influences whether exposure is likely to be effective is the extent to which the exposures are predictable. Unfortunately, animals are by nature unpredictable. They can often surprise you with their movements and the sounds they make. Before beginning each practice, it is a good idea to make sure that the animal you are using is unlikely to surprise you. For example, it is better to start off with a relatively calm dog than a hyper dog. Furthermore, we recommend starting with the animal restrained. For example, a dog should be on a leash, a cockroach should be in a jar, and a bird should be in a cage. Later in your treatment, it may be useful to practice with animals that are less predictable, such as birds that flap their wings and make a lot of noise or snakes that are active.

long exposures are the key to success

When overcoming any fear, longer exposures tend to be more effective than briefer exposures. Practices that are too brief provide all the disadvantages of exposure with none of the advantages. They trigger fear and panic, but they're too short to provide an opportunity for the fear to naturally subside. In fact, if you leave the situation when your fear is at its peak, you will reinforce your belief that being around your feared animal is terrifying and that escaping leads to a reduction in fear. Only by staying in the feared situation until your fear decreases will you learn that you can be around the animal and not be afraid.

Your fear will decrease over time, but it may take a while. Plan for exposure practices that last at least sixty minutes and preferably ninety minutes to two hours. Try to stay with the practice until your fear has decreased or until you have been able to increase the intensity of the practice (by moving closer to the animal, for example) without your fear becoming overwhelming.

schedule your practices close together

If your practices are too spread out, each practice will feel like you are starting all over again. Ideally, you should practice on a daily basis until even the item at the top of your hierarchy no longer arouses fear. By making sure that your exposures are close together, the practices will build on one another and you will experience a greater reduction in fear. If you cannot practice on a daily basis, make sure that you do find the time to practice at least several times per week at the start. Once your fear has decreased significantly, it may be useful to continue occasional exposures from time to time in order to pre-vent your fear from returning. At this later stage, it will be fine for these "booster" exposures to be more spread out. The steps to preventing a return of fear after success-ful exposure therapy are covered in chapter 7.

eliminate safety behaviors

Safety behaviors can interfere with the benefits of exposure. Therefore, it is important to gradually eliminate these behaviors over the course of your treatment. If you find it necessary to use some of these behaviors during early exposures, that's fine. However, as your fear decreases, try to reduce your reliance on any unnecessary overprotective behaviors. Here are some examples of behaviors to consider gradually eliminating over the course of your treatment:

◊   Sitting near the door when visiting friends who have a dog (just in case you need to run out of the room)

◊   Going to sleep with the lights on (just in case you are woken up by a cockroach and need to find it quickly)

◊   Checking the inside of the car thoroughly before getting in (to make sure there are no spiders inside)

◊   Avoiding looking inside pet stores (just in case they sell mice)

Again, you can refer back to chapter 1 for a longer list of examples.

practice in different situations and with different animals

Often, people who fear animals also fear the environments in which they tend to encounter those animals. For example, if you are afraid of dogs, you may also be afraid of going into parks, walking around your neighborhood, visiting certain friends, and walking by pet stores. If you are afraid of bugs, you may find parks, gardens, basements, and attics scary. As you begin to confront your feared animal, be sure to expose yourself to the animal in a wide range of places where there is an increased likelihood of encountering it (for example, you might work with cats at a local pet store, at your cousin's home, and at the Humane Society). By exposing yourself to the different contexts in which you tend to encounter your feared animal, your fear of these places will also decrease.

Also, it is best to practice with a variety of different animals. For example, if you are afraid of snakes and you do all your exposure with a particular snake, you may learn to be comfortable with that particular snake but not with others. Working with three or four different animals (for example, several different dogs) will ensure that your reduction in fear is not limited to only a particular animal (your neighbor's dog).

don't fight your fear

If you become frightened during an exposure practice, do not look at your fear as a sign of weakness or as an indication that the practice is going poorly. In fact, experiencing fear is a sign that the exposure is going exactly as planned. Don't fight your fear when it occurs. Just let it happen. It's fine if your heart races, if you sweat, become breathless, cry, or scream during exposure. The more you try to fight your fear, the longer it will take your fear to decrease. Letting your fear happen is like riding a wave. Keep in mind that your fear will peak and then pass—you just have to wait it out.

protect yourself from real danger

Exposures should never involve doing anything that most people would consider dangerous. For example, it is unwise to handle dogs with a history of biting or snakes that you stumble across while hiking outdoors. If you live in an area where there are dangerous spiders, be sure to know something about the spiders you are using before handling them. Ordering your spiders from a biological supply company (see chapter 4) is one way to ensure that the spiders you are using are safe. When working with larger animals like dogs and cats, make sure they are comfortable being around people, to avoid the possibility of being bitten or scratched. If you are working with someone's pet, it may be helpful to have the pet's owner present during the practices. Over years of working with clients with animal phobias, we have never had a person be attacked by their feared animal during the therapy. Still, it is better to be safe than sorry.

how to know when treatment is complete

Your treatment can come to an end when your fear is minimal, even when practicing the item at the top of your hierarchy. Ideally, your exposures should continue until you can handle your feared animal comfortably (holding a snake, having a spider crawling on your hand, hugging a friendly dog). You may be thinking, "Why should I handle my feared animal? I don't need to be able to actually handle the animal in my everyday life." It is important to take the exposure as far as possible for two reasons. First, taking the exposure to the extreme ensures that any remaining belief that the animal is dangerous is thoroughly challenged. Second, if you don't encounter the feared animal for a long time, there is a chance that some of your fear will return. If you take the exposure practices far enough, some of your fear may return, but it will not begin to interfere again with your life.

exposure case examples

This section describes the use of exposure to treat particular animal phobias, including fears of spiders and crawling insects, moths, dogs, and snakes. Each case illustrates the specific treatment program that was used, which should make it easier for you to develop a program for overcoming your fear, based on your own hierarchy. Although the treatment of other animal fears (such as fears of cats, birds, lizards, and rodents) is not described in detail, the cases presented in this section should provide you with enough information to set up an exposure program for almost any excessive animal fear.

Karen—spiders and crawling insects

Karen had been afraid of spiders for as long as she could recall. She was equally afraid of certain types of crawling insects, including centipedes, cockroaches, earwigs, and beetles. Her fear had gotten worse in recent years since she had moved to a more rural area. Karen's fear was moderate. She was okay being in the same room as a spider or feared insect as long as it was in a sealed jar (for example, her fear level was initially 80 on a scale of 0 to 100 if she looked at a spider in a jar from about three feet away, but she could do it). Because she was able to be relatively close to a spider, her exposure practices began with doing just that. There was no need to start with pictures of spiders or toy insects because she was able to get close to the real thing. One of her husband's coworkers found a medium-sized, harmless spider in his basement for Karen to use in treatment.

Karen initially spent about fifteen minutes looking at the spider in a sealed jar. Her husband held the jar so Karen could see inside. The lid of the jar had several holes in it, so the spider could breathe, and there was a small stick in the jar, so the spider could spin webs and crawl around. After fifteen minutes, Karen's fear decreased to a level of 40. She was ready to move closer to the jar. When she was about a foot away from the jar, her fear level increased to 80 again. After about ten minutes, her fear was down to a 40.

The next step was for Karen to touch the outside of the jar while her husband held it. Her fear shot up to about a 90 when she touched the jar. However, she continued to touch the jar, while looking at the spider inside. When her fear had decreased again, to about a level of 50, Karen decided that she was ready to hold the jar. Again, her fear increased temporarily and gradually decreased to a level of 30 over about five minutes. Karen felt good about her progress, but she decided to take a break until the next day. She was exhausted.

The following day, she and her husband started with her holding the jar again. Although her fear was higher at first, within about five minutes it decreased to a level of 30. She was now ready to try exposure to the spider outside of the jar. She moved back to about six feet away, while her husband released the spider into a large, clear plastic tub. Karen's fear was close to a 90 when the spider was released. Her husband sat in a chair with the tub on his lap. As the spider attempted to crawl up the sides of the tub, he tapped it gently back to the bottom of the tub. He had no problem making sure that the spider remained in the tub.

Over the next half hour, Karen's fear gradually decreased, and she got closer and closer to the spider, until she was standing about a foot away from it, with only mild fear. Next, she practiced getting closer to actually touching the spider. She touched the inside of the tub and also touched the spider with the end of a pencil. Although these steps were quite difficult at first, they gradually became easier. Within about twenty minutes, Karen was able to quickly touch the spider. When she first touched the spider, her fear level hit 100—the highest it had been since the treatment began. Again, Karen was exhausted, and she began to cry. She had had enough for one day. At that point, her husband suggested that she step back about one foot from the spider and asked her how strong her fear was. She realized that her fear was only about a 10 out of 100 from that distance. Although touching the spider was very difficult, it was clear just how far she had come in just a short time.

The next day, Karen and her husband began where they had left off the day before. She immediately started trying to touch the spider. Again, her fear was very high, but she was determined to continue the exposure, despite the fear. Within about fifteen minutes, she was able to touch the spider with only mild levels of fear. Next, her husband lifted the spider by the leg and touched the spider to Karen's open palm. The goal was to see how long Karen could keep the spider on her hand. At first, she tossed the spider off her hand into the tub immediately. After the third or fourth time, however, she was able to keep the spider on her hand for a few seconds. After about ten minutes of practicing holding the spider, she tried picking up the spider herself (using a business card) and then passing the spider from hand to hand. Karen's fear was down to a 30 after about ten more minutes of exposure. She was thrilled with her progress. They decided to call it a day and went out for dinner to celebrate.

Karen took the next couple of days off from practicing. Then she and her husband began to work with other spiders and insects. Her husband was able to get a cockroach from a biology researcher at a local university, and they were able to catch an earwig in the garage. They also found a spider in their neighbor's backyard. Karen practiced looking at her new "friends" one at a time, first from a distance of about three feet and then up close. Within about an hour, she was able to hold each of them with a fear level of about 10. To test herself, she tried handling bugs and spiders in her basement and in her garden—two places she tended to avoid in the past. Both of these practices were now easy for her.

Essentially, Karen had overcome her fear. Over the coming months, she practiced catching insects in jars and releasing them outside whenever she encountered them in her home. If she encountered spiders that were particularly large or that she thought might be poisonous, she was able to kill them, though she still felt somewhat frightened.

Shannon—moths

Shannon's fear of moths began in childhood. Although she had no recollection of how it began, her older sister was also scared of moths, and Shannon wondered whether she had learned the fear from her sister. For years, Shannon was able to live with her fear. It wasn't until she was an adult and had begun camping on weekends that the fear became a real problem. Her fear also prevented her from sitting in her backyard at night.

The first step for Shannon was to have someone catch several moths to use in the treatment. Because moths are attracted to light, they were easy to catch in her backyard at night by turning off her house lights and leaving the porch light on. When a moth landed on the porch lamp, her roommate Ashley was able to catch it in a jar. Ashley agreed to help Shannon with her exposures.

Shannon's treatment began in the same way that Karen's treatment for spider phobia did (we recommend that you read Karen's story if you haven't already done so). Shannon initially practiced looking at the moth in a jar held by Ashley. Within about thirty minutes, Shannon went from looking at the jar from about six feet away to looking at it from only a foot away. Over the next half hour, Shannon practiced touching the jar and eventually holding it. Her fear decreased from a level of 90 when she first touched the jar to a level of 50 while holding the jar. Although her fear was still moderately high, she felt ready to move to the next step—exposure to a loose moth.

Moths are quite a bit more difficult to control than spiders. Shannon and Ashley considered three possibilities that would allow some degree of control over the moth. First, they considered releasing the moth into an old five gallon fish tank with plastic wrap over the top. That way, they could each put their hands in the tank (through a hole in the plastic) without having the moth escape. The other option they considered was to clear out a small, well-lit closet so they could be in the closet with the moth and the moth would not be able to get away. The third option was to practice exposure to moths outside, near the porch light, where they tended to gather at night.

Shannon decided to practice outside initially. Knowing that she could run away if a moth flew toward her gave her a sense of control in the situation. Shannon practiced standing near the porch light for about fifteen minutes, until her fear decreased from an 80 to about a 40. Then, with Shannon's permission, Ashley touched the moths on the light to see if she could get them to fly around. Shannon's fear level shot up to 100 briefly, but it gradually decreased as Ashley continued to keep the moths moving. More than two hours had passed since Shannon's treatment began. She had made outstanding progress, but she was ready for a break.

A couple of days later, Shannon and Ashley resumed their practices. This time, Ashley caught a moth and placed it in the covered fish tank. At first, Ashley placed her hand in the tank (through the plastic cover), modeling the procedure for Shannon. Next, Shannon did the same thing, at first making sure that her hand didn't touch the moth. After about thirty minutes, however, Shannon was able to touch the moth inside the fish tank. Next, they released the moth into the small closet and both stood in the closet with the moth. Shannon's fear was quite low by this point, even though the moth was flying around. After about ten minutes, Shannon was able to catch the moth in a jar and release it in her backyard. Shannon had successfully overcome her phobia. She no longer feared encountering moths in her backyard or while camping with friends.

Louis—dogs

When Louis was twelve years old, he was bitten by a German shepherd while visiting a friend's home. His wound healed quickly, but his fear of being bitten again only increased as he got older. He had difficulty walking around his neighborhood alone and he was unable to visit the home of his girlfriend, who owned a Labrador retriever. Although he was fearful of all dogs, his fear was worse with large dogs, dogs that had a reputation for being aggressive, and dogs that tended to bark a lot.

With his girlfriend's help, Louis decided to start his exposure with puppies from the local pet store. He had no problem looking at the puppies behind the glass, so his girlfriend asked the store clerk whether they could play with a puppy on a leash. As long as his girlfriend was holding the leash and Louis was standing more than six feet away from the dog, his fear was manageable. He decided to try standing about three feet away. He rated his fear level to be at 80 from that distance. After about ten minutes, it was down to a 50. The store was getting busy and the clerk requested that the dog be returned to its cage. Louis and his girlfriend agreed to find another dog for their next practice.

In the meantime, Louis started spending more time in places where he might see dogs. He and his girlfriend took daily walks in his neighborhood, including the local park where people often walked their dogs. Although he normally crossed the road whenever he saw a dog, he made every effort to continue walking on the same side, even if it meant getting close to a dog. However, he continued to cross the road if he saw a dog that wasn't on a leash.

Next, Louis arranged to visit with a close friend who happened to own a beagle. His friend had agreed to spend about ninety minutes working with Louis and the dog. Although Louis was embarrassed by his fear, the friend was delighted to help out. Louis began by standing about three feet from the dog while the friend held on to the leash. Over a period of fifteen minutes, his fear decreased from an 80 to a 30. He gradually worked on getting close to the dog. Next, his friend agreed to hold the dog while Louis touched the dog's back. Though his fear level was very high, Louis felt some reassurance when he saw the dog's tail wag as he stroked its back. He continued to practice touching the dog's back for another twenty minutes until his fear decreased from a level of 90 to a level of 40. When he was ready, Louis then tried to stroke the dog's head. Before trying this step, he asked his friend to do it a few times to see how the dog would react. His friend reassured Louis that the dog enjoyed being touched, and he touched the dog as Louis requested. Then, Louis touched the dog's head a few times and found that his fear decreased quickly.

Louis's girlfriend was surprised when he called her a few days later to say that he wanted to meet her dog before the two of them went off to see a movie. He was quite nervous about meeting the dog because it was relatively large. Initially, they began with the dog on a leash. It took Louis about ten minutes to be able to touch the dog's back while his girlfriend held the dog's head. After another ten minutes, Louis was able to touch the dog's head. His fear seemed to decrease very quickly. Next, he decided to allow the dog off the leash. Though he was quite nervous initially, it quickly became easier. The dog was fairly calm and Louis's fear was greatly reduced. He now had little fear of his girlfriend's dog, and he started to visit her house on a more regular basis.

Louis continued to work on his fear about three days per week. Over the course of the next two weeks, he was able to practice being around a number of large dogs. He practiced handling dogs belonging to friends and relatives. He also touched dogs that he passed while walking outside (with the owner's permission), and he no longer crossed the road when he saw a loose dog. As a final step, he went to the Humane Society and practiced touching a German shepherd until his fear was minimal.

Charlene—snakes

Charlene grew up in a small town with a single school, where every student knew everyone else. Among other things, the other students were well aware that Charlene was terrified of snakes. For years, the boys in her school frequently teased her with snakes, and on several occasions they put live snakes down her top and in her school bag. Charlene lived with her fear for years. By the time she decided to seek treatment, she was in her mid-thirties, was married, and had two children. She decided to get help when her oldest son turned five years old. She was worried that he might start catching snakes and bringing them home—her worst nightmare.

Charlene's fear was severe. She avoided all situations where she might see snakes, including walking through wooded areas and watching nature shows on television. She refused to see a movie unless she checked to see whether there were any snakes in the film. She couldn't look at pictures of snakes (including cartoons). Even saying the word "snake" made her anxious. When she first sought treatment, Charlene experienced nightmares about snakes approximately twice per week.

Charlene refused to look at a live snake or even at a picture of a snake at the start of her treatment, so she and her therapist began treatment by having her simply repeat the word "snake." That practice became fairly easy within about fifteen minutes, so they increased the intensity of the exposure. Next, Charlene practiced saying "slithery snake." This was considerably more difficult, but again it became easier within a few minutes.

Despite feeling very apprehensive, Charlene decided that she would try looking at a small cartoon drawing of a snake with a smiling face. Her initial fear level began at about 90 and decreased to a level of 60 over the course of the next hour. Charlene was feeling some sense of accomplishment, but she was also quite discouraged at how far she still had to go. She agreed to look at the cartoon snake for about thirty minutes each day over the next week.

When Charlene saw her therapist the following week, her fear of the cartoon snake was down to a level of 5. She was also still very comfortable saying the phrase "slithery snake." So, she and her therapist moved up to the next item on her hierarchy—looking at photographs of snakes. At first, her fear level was close to 100 again. Over the next hour and a half, she practiced looking at photos of several different snakes. By the end of the session, she was able to touch the photos. Her fear was still at a level of about 50, but she was beginning to feel good about the gains that she had made.

Over the next week, Charlene practiced looking at her pictures of snakes for homework. Although her fear was decreasing with each day that went by, she noticed a dramatic increase in snake-related dreams when she slept. In fact, the dreams were now occurring almost every night. At her next therapy session, Charlene began by touching more photos of snakes. It was apparent that her fear of photos had decreased—even with the most vivid photos, her fear level was at 20. She spent the rest of the session looking at, touching, and eventually holding a number of toy snakes made from rubber or plastic. She seemed to be most frightened by a large black rubber snake that looked quite real. Although her fear of the other toy snakes subsided rather quickly, her fear of the large black snake was still at about a 70 after more than a half hour of handling it. Charlene agreed to practice handling the large rubber snake daily over the next week.

Again, Charlene's fear continued to decrease as she practiced her exposure homework. At her next therapy session, she agreed to look at a live snake. Charlene and her therapist arranged to pay the manager of a local pet store a small fee to stay for two hours after the store had closed. At first, Charlene could only stand near the front of the store. Although she could not see any snakes from where she was standing, just knowing that they were in the store caused her fear to rise. After about ten minutes, she agreed to look at a snake in an aquarium from a distance of about twenty feet. It was not as scary as she anticipated, so she moved to a distance of about ten feet. From that distance, her fear was at a level of about 70 and she decided to move closer. At about five feet away from the snake, her fear level jumped to about 90 and then to 100, when she thought she saw the snake move. Charlene practiced looking at the snake for about one hour; eventually she was able to touch the outside of the aquarium with only moderate fear.

Charlene spent the next week visiting the pet store (during regular business hours) and looking at snakes through the aquarium glass. Her nightmares had completely stopped. For her next treatment session, she and her therapist made arrangements for the pet store manager to stay late again. This time, they worked on handling live snakes. At first, the manager held the snake with the head facing away from Charlene, which allowed Charlene and her therapist to practice touching the tail end of the snake. Reluctantly, Charlene complied. Over the next hour, she reached a point at which she could hold the tail end of the snake while the manager firmly held the rest of the snake. Charlene could not believe that she was actually holding a snake.

Charlene's treatment included two additional sessions, each lasting about ninety minutes. Over the course of these sessions, Charlene practiced gradually holding more and more of the snake until she could hold the entire snake. She repeated the practice with several other snakes. By the end of her last session, her fear while holding the largest snake in the store (about four feet long) was at about a 30. Though she could not believe what she was saying, Charlene reported that she now found snakes interesting and enjoyed handling them, despite still feeling mildly frightened.

EXERCISE: Practice Exposure to Your Feared Animal

This is the most important (and perhaps the most difficult) exercise described in this book. It is this exercise that will help you to overcome your animal fear. Doing this will take time, patience, and a willingness to feel uncomfortable initially. Essentially, the exercise involves repeatedly confronting your feared animal until you are no longer afraid.

Use the strategies described throughout this chapter (as well as the preparation you completed in chapters 3 and 4) to design the most appropriate program for dealing with your fear. The case examples provided in this chapter illustrate how you might organize your own exposure practices. Remember, exposures should be planned, structured, predictable, prolonged, and frequent. Try to use several different animals from your feared species, and practice in different locations where you tend to encounter your feared animal. Keep repeating this exercise until you can handle the animal comfortably.

Each time you conduct an exposure practice, record in your journal what steps you were able to complete (for example, standing four feet from a mouse in a cage, standing one foot from a mouse in a cage, putting your hand in a cage containing a mouse, touching the mouse with a gloved hand, touching the mouse with a bare hand, holding the mouse). For each step, record your fear level every five or ten minutes. This will allow you to assess changes in your fear over time. Use a scale ranging from 0 to 100, where 0 equals no fear and 100 equals maximum fear.

troubleshooting

Unfortunately, exposure practices don't always go as smoothly as you might like. Here are some problems that sometimes arise and some suggestions for overcoming each one.

finding time to practice

One of the biggest challenges in exposure therapy is finding the time to practice. Again, we suggest that you schedule your practices in your date book the way you would any other important activity. You may find that you need to clear your schedule to make it happen. For instance, if you have children at home, you may need to hire a babysitter. If you work during the week, you may be able to do exposures on weekends and evenings, but you may also find it easier to complete your exposure practices if you take a few days off work and make exposure your full-time job on those days. Regardless of where you find the time, it usually doesn't take long to overcome an animal fear or phobia. By juggling a few things in your schedule, it should be possible to get the job done.

dealing with unpredictable animals

As mentioned earlier, it is best to work with animals that are likely to behave in predictable ways, especially early in treatment. It is ideal to use animals that are comfortable around people and that are unlikely to bite, make a lot of noise, or run away. Of course, this may be difficult with certain types of animals. For example, flying insects and birds are unlikely to sit still while you try to overcome your fear. The key in these cases is to find creative ways to restrain the animal. Shannon's case illustrated how this can be accomplished with moths. If you are working with birds, you may need to use birds in cages or pigeons that are used to being around people on city streets, to avoid the problem of the animal getting away. A large parrot in a pet store can provide an opportunity to get close to a larger bird without it flying away. Later in treatment, it may be useful to have contact with birds that move around a lot and make lots of noise (in pet stores or in parks).

If an unpredictable event occurs (for example, if a spider gets away during an exposure), try to stay focused. Unpredictable events may lead to an increase in fear, but don't let them undermine your progress overall. Try to get back on track with your exposure practices as soon as possible.

what to do when fear won't come down

Exposure may not always lead to a reduction in your fear. If you find that your fear doesn't come down during exposure practices, consider the following possible explanations and solutions:

◊ The practice is too difficult and the fear is too overwhelming, so you can't even focus on what you are doing. If this is the case, try an easier exposure.

◊ Not enough time has elapsed. Remember, it may take an hour or two to notice a decrease in fear in some cases. Try staying in the situation longer.

⬧ You are engaging in subtle avoidance.
   Using safety behaviors during exposure may
   interfere with fear reduction over the
   course of an exposure practice.

⬧ The animal is behaving unpredictably. If
   the animal is moving around a lot, making
   noise, or doing other unpredictable things
   that increase your fear, it may take longer
   for your fear to come down.

⬧ You are having a bad day. During times of
   stress, exposure to animals will likely be
   more difficult. If your fear isn't coming
   down, either because of general life stress
   or for reasons of which you are unaware, try
   again on another day. If it is still too difficult, it may be a good idea to enlist a helper
   (if you are trying it on your own) or to seek
   professional help.

overcoming fears of dangerous animals

Sometimes, people fear animals that truly are dangerous, but their fear is out of proportion to the actual
threat. For example, although most people have a healthy
respect for sharks, poisonous snakes, bees, and venomous
spiders, for some people, fear occurs even in places that
are perfectly safe. If this describes you, you'll be relieved
to hear that we don't recommend you touch and hold the

animal. However, we do recommend that you expose yourself to the places or situations that you avoid—especially if they are situations that most people wouldn't avoid. For example, if you are afraid of bees, we suggest that you practice eating in outdoor cafés or working in your garden, despite the possibility of encountering bees. If you see a bee, try to stay in the situation. In other words, try to behave the way someone might act if he or she didn't have a fear of bees. If you are allergic to bee stings, you will want to be more careful. For example, make sure you have the proper treatment on hand (such as an Epipen for injecting epinephrine), just in case.

Summary

Exposure is the only treatment that has repeatedly been shown to reduce the fear of animals. Exposure works best when it is predictable, controlled, frequent, and prolonged. It is useful to take increasingly difficult steps as quickly as you are willing to take them and to eliminate safety behaviors during practices. In addition to describing strategies for practicing exposure, this chapter provided detailed exposure case examples for fears of spiders, moths, dogs, and snakes. It also discussed how to solve some of the problems that can arise during exposure practices.

6

changing your thoughts

Fear is the body's natural response to *perceived* danger or threat. In other words, you become frightened when you *believe* that a particular object or situation is dangerous. Sometimes these beliefs are accurate, as is the case with realistic fears. However, in the case of phobias, beliefs tend to be exaggerated, biased, or even completely untrue. An important goal of treatment is to help you to interpret the object of your fear in a more balanced and realistic way. In the case of animal phobias, exposure to the feared situation is the most powerful way of discovering that it is in fact safe (see chapter 5). This chapter discusses some additional strategies for challenging the beliefs that contribute to your fear. Together, the techniques in this chapter are often referred to as *cognitive* strategies (the word "cognition" just refers to the process of thinking).

Although there is almost no research examining the use of cognitive strategies for animal phobias, there is considerable research supporting these techniques for treating other types of fear and anxiety-based conditions (such as social anxiety and panic attacks). By examining the evidence for their anxious thoughts, people with anxiety-based problems are able to replace negative thinking patterns with more realistic interpretations and beliefs, thereby decreasing their fear and anxiety in frightening situations. In the case of animal fears, almost all of the studies to date have been on exposure-based treatments, as described in chapter 5. In the end, it is the extent to which you practice the exposure strategies that will probably determine how successful you are at overcoming your fear. Nevertheless, you may find the cognitive techniques described in this chapter to be useful as a way of dealing with anxious beliefs that get in the way of your exposure practices.

People are often unaware of the specific thoughts, beliefs, and assumptions that underlie their fears. In many cases, the thoughts seem to occur so quickly and automatically that they remain outside of awareness. Still, many experts believe that fear often occurs in response to an assumption (either conscious or unconscious) that a particular situation poses a threat. In addition to helping you identify and change your anxious thoughts, cognitive strategies can also help you become more aware of the biased ways in which you may seek out knowledge, pay attention to information, and remember events. Later, the chapter will cover how to use cognitive strategies to manage your fear, but first, here is a review of the scientific evidence regarding the role of attention, memory, and thinking in maintaining animal fears.

what science tells us

Over the past few decades, psychology researchers have been very interested in the role of thinking, attention, and memory in causing and maintaining problems with anxiety and fear. Because animal phobias are so common, many researchers have chosen to investigate these processes in people who suffer from these fears, especially fears of spiders. Some of the most important findings to emerge from this body of research include the following:

◊   People with spider phobias are more likely than people without spider phobias to overestimate the likelihood of being bitten by a spider and for the likelihood that injuries will result from being bitten (Jones, Whitmont, and Menzies 1996).

◊   People with spider and snake phobias tend to overestimate the degree of activity in their feared animal (in other words, how much the animal moves around), though this perceptual distortion tends to be corrected following treatment (Rachman and

Cuk 1992). People with spider phobias also tend to believe that spiders selectively move toward them, rather than toward other people in the same area (Riskind, Moore, and Bowley 1995).

◇ People with spider phobias tend to remember details from photos of spiders better than they remember details from other types of photos (Wessel and Merckelbach 1998).

◇ Though a few studies have failed to show any biases in attention, a number have found that people with spider phobias tend to pay more attention to information related to their fear (to spider-related words or pictures of spiders) than do people without spider phobias. Also, although results are mixed, some studies have shown that treatment for animal phobias leads to a normalizing of attentional biases (Antony and Barlow 2002).

◇ When people with spider phobias are exposed to spiders, they tend to focus not only on the spider but also on objects that represent safety, such as the door (Thorpe and Salkovskis 1998).

what does the research mean for you?

Overall, the research literature supports the notion that people with animal phobias tend to process information in a way that supports their anxious beliefs. This means that, compared to people without phobias, you may be more likely to view your feared animal as dangerous, to remember information in a biased way (for example, that a spider was moving very quickly), and to seek out and pay attention to threat-related triggers. However, the findings should be interpreted with caution for two reasons. First, as with any area of research, the studies described earlier have inconsistent results (some found differences between people with phobias and people without phobias, and others didn't), perhaps because of the different research methods used. Second, most of the research on cognition and animal phobias has been based on spider phobias. We assume that the results might look similar in people with fears of birds, dogs, cats, snakes, and other animals. However, it is impossible to know for sure.

Do you notice a tendency in yourself to pay extra attention to information related to the animal you fear? For example, if you hear someone talking about dogs, do your ears perk up? If there is a spider in the room, are you always the first person to notice it? Do you sometimes mistake sticks on the ground for snakes? Do you remember the details of past encounters with cats like they just happened yesterday? Do you tend to view birds as more dangerous than other people you know do? If your answer to questions such as these is yes, then it may be that your thinking, attention, and memory are biased in a way that serves to maintain your fear over time. Changing your thinking habits may help to reduce your fear.

figuring out what you're thinking

Before you can begin to change your anxious thoughts, you must first try to identify their content. What are you afraid will happen if you encounter your feared animal? People typically have thoughts concerning danger from the animal itself (for example, a fear of being bitten), but they may also have anxiety over their own reactions to the animal (such as a fear of embarrassing themselves in front of others, or a fear of passing out). Here are some common anxious thoughts that we have observed among people with animal fears:

thoughts about the feared animal

◊ *The animal will bite, scratch, or hurt me.*

◊ *The animal will attack me because it can tell I am scared.*

◊ *The animal will touch me (for example—the spider will crawl on me; the cat will jump on me; the dog will lick me).*

◊ *The animal will move toward me.*

◊   *The animal is mean and nasty.*

◊   *The animal is contaminated and will make me sick.*

thoughts about your reaction to the animal

◊   *I will be overwhelmed with fear.*

◊   *I will be overwhelmed with disgust.*

◊   *I won't be able to cope.*

◊   *I will faint, throw up, or suffer some other physical catastrophe.*

◊   *I will make a fool of myself.*

◊   *I will lose control.*

===

EXERCISE: Identify Your Anxious Thoughts

In your journal, record your own anxious thoughts, both about the animal and about your reactions when you might encounter the animal. Do any of the sample thoughts listed above ring true for you? Are there other predictions or assumptions that cross your mind when you think about your feared animal?

---

strategies for changing anxious thoughts

To successfully change your anxious thoughts, you need to consider the possibility that your thoughts do not reflect reality. Instead of treating your thoughts as facts, think of them as hypotheses or guesses about the way things may be. Consider all of the different ways to interpret the situation. Ask yourself, "What might someone without a fear or phobia think about my feared animal?" By looking at the big picture and by examining the evidence, you will likely begin to see that your thoughts become more realistic and less anxiety provoking.

As with any new skill, the strategies described in this section require regular practice. Only with repetition will they become second nature.

educating yourself

Often, phobias are associated with misinformation about the feared animal. For example, people who fear dogs may overestimate the chances of getting bitten. They may see dogs as a much bigger threat than most other sources of danger. Here are some statistics off a

Web site (Phillips 1999) designed to warn people about the dangers of being bitten by dogs. As you review this information, be careful not to focus only on the most frightening aspects. Although these figures may seem scary in isolation, when put in a larger context, the information may help to alleviate your fears. Based on 1994 statistics, more than a third of American households owned a dog, and the dog population in the United States was over fifty-two million. Assuming these statistics haven't changed much since 1994, the average American has only a one in fifty chance of being bitten in a given year. Fewer than one million Americans are bitten by dogs each year, and most of these are children. About one in six (133,333) dog bites requires medical attention (or one in twelve, if we consider only adults who are bitten). The number of people who die each year from dog attacks is about three hundred, of which almost all are children. For every fatal dog attack in the United States, there are 230,000 that don't even require treatment by a physician.

Depending on your perspective, the risk of being bitten may sound high based on these statistics. After all, 133,000 people needing medical attention from a dog bite is a big number! However, the risks of being bitten by a dog are in line with many other risks that confront us every day. Consider these figures from the Centers for Disease Control on the number of Americans treated in emergency rooms for various nonfatal injuries during the year 2002 (National Center for Injury Prevention and Control):

Number of People	Type of Injury
7,410,159	Unintentional falls
4,490,051	Being unintentionally struck
3,286,856	Unintentional overexertion
2,988,064	Unintentional motor vehicle accident
2,278,105	Being unintentionally cut
1,270,224	Being intentionally struck (in other words, an assault)
880,910	Bites or stings from animals other than dogs

Here are some other U.S. statistics that we found on the Internet:

354,670	Number of women who were raped in 1995 (Paralumun New Age Women's Village)
6,316,000	Number of car accidents in 2002 (car-accidents.com 2004)
2,900,000	Number of injuries from car accidents in 2002 (car-accidents.com 2004)

3,500,000	Number of sports-related injuries each year for children under fourteen (University of Maryland Medical System 2003)
600,000	Number of bicycle-related accidents leading to emergency room visits (University of Maryland Medical System 2003)

So dog bites are far less common than many other unfortunate events. Also, using common sense can often help to prevent dog attacks. A number of factors appear to influence risk. According to the Web site www.dog bitelaw.com, more than three-quarters of dog bite victims are children, with the highest rate of attacks for children between the ages of five and nine. Almost four out of five biting dogs belong to the victim's family or friend. These statistics suggest that children should be particularly careful but that adults are at a relatively low risk of being bitten, particularly by unfamiliar dogs.

So, what's the point of all these statistics? The point is that doing a bit of research can help to provide information that can put your fear in perspective. Educating yourself may involve trying to find out just how dangerous your feared animal is, or it may involve learning more about the animal in general. Good sources of information include the Internet and educational books and videos. However, don't believe everything you hear. People who publish books and produce Web sites often have an agenda. For example, Web sites by dog enthusiasts may underestimate the risks associated with dogs, whereas sites by victims of dog attacks may overemphasize the risks of being bitten.

Here are some questions you might want to answer through a bit of research:

⬧ *Do most spiders bite? What will I feel if I am bitten by a spider? Under what conditions do spiders bite?*

According to one source, about 80 percent of suspected spider bites are actually not caused by spiders but rather are caused by fleas, lice, mosquitoes, biting flies, ants, and other small animals (Harris).

⬧ *Why does a snake stick its tongue out? Is it a sign that the snake is about to attack? What do snakes eat? How do snakes like to be handled? What does it feel like to handle a snake?*

⬧ *Can birds really tell that I'm afraid? Are they more likely to fly toward me if I am afraid?*

⬧ *How likely is a mouse from a pet store to bite me? Do mice sold as pets spread diseases?*

EXERCISE: Learn About Your Feared Animal

Are there things about your animal that you would like to find out? In your journal, record a list of questions about your feared animal. Now, set out to answer your questions. Pick up a good book on the animal, or do your research on the Internet. Be careful not to selectively give more weight to information that confirms your anxious thoughts. Try to use a balanced approach when deciding which information is most useful.

challenging probability overestimations

Overestimating probabilities involves predicting that a particular event is more likely to occur than it really is. Examples of such overestimations include statements such as these:

◊   *The bird will attack me.*

◊   *The spider will bite me.*

◊   *I will die if I have to be in the same room as a cat.*

Although there a remote chance that some of these things could come true, in reality, birds almost never attack people, spiders rarely bite, and I cannot think of anyone who has ever died from seeing a harmless animal, no matter how strong their fear was. The belief that an event such as one of these is likely to occur is an example of a *probability overestimation*.

The key to combating probability overestimations is to examine the evidence for and against your beliefs. After considering all of the available information, you will be in a better position to come to a more realistic conclusion. Remember, because of a tendency to pay more attention to information that confirms your anxious beliefs, coming up with evidence supporting your phobic predictions may come more naturally at first. With practice, generating evidence contradicting your anxious thoughts will become easier. In order to examine the evidence, it is useful to ask yourself a series of questions:

◊   *Do I know for certain that my fears will come true?*

◊   *What does my past experience tell me about this situation? Have I made similar predictions in the past? Did they come true?*

◊   *What do the statistics suggest?*

◊   *How might someone who is not afraid think about this situation?*

The goal of asking these questions is to help you to think about your feared animal in a more realistic way, based on having considered the evidence for and against your fearful predictions. Here is an example of how to challenge the belief that you will be attacked by a cat:

⋄ **Anxious belief:** "The cat will attack me if I get too close."

⋄ **Evidence in support of belief:** "Cats are unpredictable. It's hard to know what they're thinking. I've heard of a few occasions when cats have attacked people. I have also had two different cats hiss at me in the past. Perhaps they would have tried to bite me if I didn't move away."

⋄ **Evidence against belief:** "I learned on the Internet that there are more than twenty million pet cats in the United States and another sixty to one hundred million stray or wild cats. Yet, I almost never hear of people being attacked by cats, with a couple of exceptions. Even if a cat were to bite someone, I imagine the attack would typically happen in response to the cat being provoked, teased, or frightened. I am much bigger than a cat—if one were to attack me, I would be able to protect myself."

⋄ **Rational conclusion:** "In reality, I am very unlikely to be attacked by a cat. Even if a cat did try to attack me, I would easily get control of the situation. The worst thing that would happen is that I would be startled and shaken up. If I were bitten, the wound would heal quickly."

EXERCISE: Examine the Evidence

In your journal, record an example of a probability overestimation that sometimes crosses your mind when thinking about your feared animal. Next, record the evidence in support of the belief, the evidence against the belief, and your rational conclusion, based on having considered all the evidence. Repeat this exercise whenever you notice yourself overestimating the threat from the animal you fear.

---

conquering catastrophic thinking

Catastrophic thinking (also called "catastrophizing") involves exaggerating the importance of a particular outcome, or incorrectly assuming that an event would be disastrous if it were to occur. This thinking style involves exaggerating how negative the impact of the event would be (as opposed to exaggerating the likelihood of the event occurring, which is the definition of probability overestimation). Examples of catastrophic thinking include the following:

◊ *If I touched a worm, I couldn't cope.*

◊ *It would be terrible to see a moth.*

◊ *If I were to see a mouse at work, I don't think I would be able to manage.*

⬧   *Even seeing a snake on television is one of the worst things I can imagine.*

Each of these examples reflects a belief that encountering the feared animal would be unmanageable if it were to happen. Of course, in reality, the only consequence of encountering these animals is likely to be temporary feelings of fear and discomfort triggered by the presence of the animal. These situations are usually much more manageable than people expect them to be.

To combat catastrophic thinking, it is useful to ask yourself questions such as:

⬧   *So what? What is the worst thing that could happen?*

⬧   *What if my feared consequence does come true?*

⬧   *How can I cope with my fear coming true?*

⬧   *Would it really be as bad as I think?*

⬧   *Would it still matter the next day? How about the next week?*

Often, by answering these questions, people discover that the situation doesn't matter nearly as much as they thought it did. Here are some examples of how you might challenge catastrophic thoughts having to do with animal fears:

◊ **Catastrophic thought:** "It would be awful if I were to see a cockroach in a movie."

◊ **Rational response:** "What would actually happen if I saw a cockroach in a movie? Well, I would feel extremely uncomfortable for a few seconds, but that's all that would happen. When I think about it that way, it doesn't seem so bad."

◊ **Catastrophic thought:** "If the bird starts squawking and flapping its wings, I won't be able to cope."

◊ **Rational response:** "So what if a bird makes a lot of noise? I am sure I would feel very frightened and startled, but it wouldn't be the first time that happened. I know from past experience that I would cope just fine. My reaction might be embarrassing if other people are around, but so what? It would pass. Everyone does embarrassing things sometimes."

◊ **Catastrophic thought:** "Seeing a live snake would be completely unmanageable."

◊ **Rational response:** "How could I cope with seeing a live snake? Chances are that I would have a panic attack and feel completely grossed out, but otherwise nothing bad would happen. After a while, my fear would subside."

EXERCISE:
Challenge Catastrophic Thinking

As you work to overcome your fear, make an effort to notice times when you engage in catastrophic thinking— or predicting that a particular outcome would be unmanageable, even though most people would not interpret the outcome in that way. In your journal, record your catastrophic thought, followed by your rational response to the thought. Practice challenging catastrophic thoughts whenever they arise.

---

troubleshooting

If you are having a hard time using the cognitive strategies described in this chapter and think you can't reduce your fear using these strategies, don't worry. Remember, exposure is almost always an effective approach for overcoming animal phobias. If you do have difficulty with cognitive techniques, however, consider the following common barriers.

inability to identify specific thoughts

Many people with animal phobias have difficulty identifying the specific beliefs, predictions, and assumptions that contribute to their fear. In many cases, their reactions seem to occur automatically, without any specific underlying thoughts. For example, most people who are afraid of earthworms know that worms are unlikely to cause any harm—no worm has ever attacked anyone. Yet the fear persists.

If you are unable to identify your thoughts, here are a few things you can try. First, give it more time. Sometimes, thoughts become more evident the more you try to become aware of them. Activating your fear may also help to make your thoughts more salient. Although it may be difficult to identify your thoughts as you read this book, you may become more aware of your thoughts upon actually being exposed to the animal. Finally, it may be easier to identify anxiety-provoking *images* that enter your mind, rather than thoughts. Are you aware of any mental images concerning the animal that you tend to experience? Again, don't worry if you can't identify your anxious beliefs or images. The exposure-based strategies discussed in chapter 5 will still work.

difficulty believing the rational thoughts

If you are successful in identifying the thoughts that contribute to your fear, you may still have difficulty believing other, more rational thoughts on an emotional level. For example, you might think, "I know rationally that the dog is unlikely to bite me, but emotionally it still feels dangerous. My head says one thing, but my heart says another."

Again, with practice you may find that your rational thoughts will become stronger and your anxious beliefs weaker. As you consider the evidence, make sure you are not giving more weight to your anxious beliefs than to an alternative, more realistic way of interpreting the situation.

Summary

Animal fears are thought to be maintained, in part, by beliefs that an animal is dangerous, as well as a tendency to pay more attention to information that confirms anxious beliefs than to information that disproves them. Although exposure is the most important strategy for overcoming animal phobias, learning to replace anxious beliefs with more realistic beliefs may help as well. In particular, learning about your feared animal, challenging probability overestimations, and countering catastrophic thinking may help to change negative thinking and increase your motivation to practice exposure.

7

staying well

As you continue to practice the exposure strategies from chapter 5 and the cognitive strategies from chapter 6, your fear will decrease until you have become comfortable around your feared animal. Once you reach this point, it is time to turn the focus to staying well—maintaining the gains that you have made, preventing a return of symptoms, and preparing for possible future episodes of fear.

what can make your fear return?

A number of factors may cause your fear to return. It is important to understand them so that you can be prepared and know how to respond. Factors that may lead to a return of your symptoms include a traumatic experience with the animal, an unexpected fear reaction, limited exposure practices during treatment, too little exposure after treatment has ended, and an increase in life stress. We will discuss each of these in turn.

traumatic experience with the animal

If you have a traumatic experience with the animal at some point in the future, your anxiety symptoms could potentially return in full force. For example, Suzy's fear of dogs returned after she was bitten by her friend's dog at a barbecue. If something like this happens to you, it doesn't mean you are back at square one. A return of fear is an understandable outcome following a traumatic experience. However, this time, you will know the strategies that you'll need to practice to reduce your fear. You may need to build a new exposure hierarchy and start engaging in exposures to reconquer your fear. You will also have the cognitive strategies you need to challenge the new anxious thoughts that may have been triggered by the traumatic experience. The good news is that because you have already tackled your fear once, it should be much faster and easier to do the second time around.

an unexpected fear reaction

Your fear could also return if at some point when you encounter the animal you experience unexpected fear symptoms or even a full-blown panic attack. For example,

Charlene had overcome her fear of snakes through the strategies that we covered in this book. Once she had finished treatment, she didn't really think much about snakes anymore. Then, several months later, a coworker surprised her by dangling a snake over her shoulder when she didn't expect it. Charlene experienced a rush of fear in response. She felt quite shaky afterward, and she was upset that she had reacted fearfully to the snake. That night, she had a bad dream in which she was chased by a snake. Charlene found that over the next few days her anxiety about snakes increased and she noticed that some of her old safety behaviors (like checking for snakes before she went into the garden) and anxious thoughts (mistaking a stick on the ground for a snake) were returning.

It is understandable that Charlene experienced a return of her anxiety after having an unexpected fear reaction to her coworker's snake "joke." Again, however, Charlene was not back at square one, and you wouldn't be either if you had an unexpected fear reaction. By resuming your exposure practices, you should be able to retackle your fears fairly quickly.

limited exposure practices during treatment

Fear may return if your exposure practices during treatment were not varied enough with respect to exposure locations, situations, and animals. For example, if you only practiced with one dog, you may find that your fear returns when you encounter different dogs. Or, if you only practiced with a mouse in a cage, your fear may return when you see a mouse running wild outdoors.

Your fear may also return if your exposure practices did not go far enough (for example, if you did not tackle all of the situations on your hierarchy, if you did not handle the animal if it was safe to do so, or you did not eliminate all of your safety behaviors). If your fear returns for one of these reasons, you will need to resume your exposure practices, this time ensuring that you vary the context and that you take your practices as far as you can go safely. You may want to enlist a helper to do this with you. You may also find it useful to review chapter 3 and construct a new hierarchy.

too little exposure after treatment has ended

Following treatment, you may find that opportunities to interact with your once-feared animal are limited. If you no longer engage in exposure practices and do not regularly encounter the animal that you were fearful of, your anxiety symptoms may gradually return. In this case, you will need to resume your exposure practices and continue to incorporate exposures to the feared animal even after your fear has subsided. For example, it is possible that if Charlene had incorporated occasional exposure to snakes into her routine (like having a snake calendar on her desk) after she had overcome her fear, she might not have responded as fearfully to her coworker's practical joke. (Some suggestions for how to incorporate exposure into your daily life appear in the next section.) Finally, remember that taking exposures to the extreme during treatment (in other words, handling a harmless spider rather than just looking at it) can provide a buffer so that if some of your fear does return, there is room for it to happen without leading to significant problems in your life.

increased life stress

For most people, life stress increases the chances of past problems returning, including insomnia, depression, excessive alcohol use, headaches, or whatever ailments may have been issues in the past. High levels of stress (work stress, relationship problems, illness, or financial difficulties) can also lead to an increase in fear among people with phobias. If you find that your fear of animals is increasing during a time of life stress, the best thing to do is to make sure that you don't fall into your old habits of relying on avoidance and safety behaviors to manage your fear. If you continue to confront your feared animal, you should find that your fear decreases again after the stress has subsided.

making sure your fear does not return

Now that you are aware of the factors that can potentially lead to a return of fear, follow the steps below to make sure that your fear does not return.

be prepared

Be prepared for a potential flare-up in your anxiety. How you respond to a traumatic experience or to an unexpected fear reaction is important in determining whether your fear will return. Getting down on yourself because of your reaction or avoiding dealing with the situation are not helpful responses and can contribute to increased anxiety. If you experience a traumatic event or an unexpected fear reaction, it is important to address your fear right away. The longer you wait, the more time you are giving your fear to build. It's okay if you experience some return of your symptoms; it just means that you will need to do some exposure practices. A return of symptoms does not mean that you are back at the beginning or that all of your hard work to overcome your fear is lost or wasted.

incorporate exposure in your life

Find ways that you can build in exposures to your animal during your normal day-to-day routine. This will help to maintain your gains and will reduce the likelihood of your fear returning. There are many options for incorporating exposures into your life:

◊   Buy books about your feared animal and keep them in places where you are likely to see them.

◊   Keep a calendar on your desk that has a different picture of your feared animal every month.

◇ Use a screensaver that has pictures of your feared animal.

◇ Visit a pet store or reptile store on a weekly basis to see your feared animal.

◇ Buy a print or picture of your feared animal that you can hang on your wall.

◇ Volunteer at your local animal or wildlife shelter.

◇ Put a picture of your feared animal on your refrigerator or mirror as a reminder of how far you have come and to make sure that you see the animal each day.

◇ Consider getting your feared animal as a pet if it is reasonable.

catch returning symptoms early and take action

Watch for a return of symptoms. If you notice that your anxiety symptoms are gradually creeping back into your life, then address the symptoms immediately. Again, ignoring the symptoms will just allow them to keep increasing. Instead, take an active approach to addressing your fear. Consider what factors may be contributing to the return of your symptoms. Have you had enough opportunities for routine exposure to your animal? Are you having some anxious thoughts about your feared animal after reading a newspaper article or seeing a program on television? Are you under increased stress? If so, are there steps that you can take to reduce your stress load? It is helpful to identify current obstacles (situations or events) that have led to a return of anxiety symptoms, as well as to anticipate future obstacles. Once you have identified the problem, you can then use your journal to make an action plan of the steps that you will take to address it. The following two cases illustrate a potential obstacle and the development of an action plan.

Carrie—fear of fish

Potential Obstacle. "I know I would like to try scuba diving on my upcoming vacation, but it could lead to a return of fear symptoms because I have never been scuba diving before and I would likely encounter fish that I have never had the chance to deal with during my exposure practices. Also, this situation would be somewhat uncontrollable as the fish may be all around me. I can feel my anxiety symptoms returning, just thinking about this."

Action Plan

1. "Education—I will learn about the types of fish I may encounter when scuba diving because then I will be more prepared for what I'll see. To do this, I'll use the Internet to go to some scuba diving Web sites. I will also talk to some of my friends who have experience with diving."

2. "Before going on the trip, I will try to examine some of my anxious thoughts about the situation. What am I afraid will happen? What is the worst thing that could happen? I'll use my cognitive strategies to consider the evidence for my fears."

3. "When I arrive for the dive, I will let the guide know that I have some anxiety. I won't be alone because I will also have my friend with me who knows about my fear. I will treat the experience like a big exposure. I'll use my cognitive strategies during the dive. I'll try to take things slowly and stay in control of the situation as best I can. As my fear decreases, I'll try to actively approach some of the fish that I see. I'll rate my fear level periodically to help me decide when to approach and when to wait until my fear has decreased."

4. "After the dive, I will consider what I learned from the experience."

Louis—fear of dogs

Potential Obstacle. "I'm planning on doing some hiking on trails when I go camping this summer. It is likely that I will encounter some big dogs that are not on leashes. It's possible that I could panic."

Action Plan. "I think that there is a good possibility that I could encounter some difficult situations. Maybe I need to do some more exposures to big dogs that are unleashed. There are some trails by my house where I could practice. I could also do some exposures at the leashless park. There are always big dogs there running around."

1. "Exposure Practice—I will practice exposures on the hiking trails by my house as well as at the leashless park."

2. "I will consider my anxious thoughts and use some of the cognitive strategies I've learned."

3. "I will be prepared to experience some fear. That's okay. I know how to handle it by using the skills that I've learned."

4. "I will focus on all the gains that I have made in overcoming my fear. I'll use this as motivation to tackle any anxiety symptoms that come up."

EXERCISE: Anticipate Obstacles and Make an Action Plan

This exercise will be helpful for identifying potential obstacles and creating an action plan that you can fall back on in case you need it. In your journal, make a list of any potential obstacles that could lead to a return of your fear. Your list may include specific situations that you have to deal with or more general triggers (like stress). For each obstacle, make an action plan for how you would deal with the obstacle should it arise. The more specific you can make your action plan, the easier it will be to follow if you need it.

Summary

A number of factors may lead to a return of your fear: traumatic experiences, unexpected fear, inadequate exposure, and stress. It is important to be prepared for future fear, to incorporate exposure into your routine, and to take action in response to a return of fear. Anticipating potential obstacles and triggers and preparing a specific action plan are steps you can take to maintain your gains, to prevent a return of fear symptoms, and to address a possible recurrence of fear in the future.

8

helping someone else
with an animal phobia

This chapter is designed for family members or others who want to help someone overcome his or her animal phobia. Being a helper is an important role. The very fact that you are reading this chapter means that you were identified as a caring and supportive person that your friend or loved one could rely on for assistance in overcoming his or her fear. It is very likely that some people would not be able to overcome their fear without the assistance of a helper. This chapter will focus on your role in treatment and the dos and don'ts of being a helper. In addition to focusing on this chapter, you may want to read the rest of the book, so you understand the basic treatment strategies and how they work.

your role as a helper

As a helper, you are there to provide support and assistance, but ultimately, the person you are helping is the one in charge. It is a good idea to sit down with the person you will be helping to discuss the role he or she would like you to play. The helper role may require you to do the following:

⬧ Provide support by listening when things get tough

⬧ Provide encouragement for continuing with the strategies

⬧ Assist in gathering materials needed for exposure practices

⬧ Help to brainstorm and set up exposure practices

⬧ Provide support during exposure practices (hold the animal, offer encouragement)

⬧ Demonstrate or model nonfearful coping behaviors during exposure practices with the feared animal

make a commitment

Agreeing to be a helper involves a time commitment of as little as a few hours on a single day to as much as a few hours on a regular basis over a period of days, weeks, or even months. The length of your time commitment will depend on the pace at which the exposure occurs. The more severe the phobia is, the longer it may take to overcome. It is a good idea to think about how you will find the time in your schedule to participate as a helper. You may need to reprioritize or juggle some of your commitments so that you don't feel stressed or overwhelmed.

make sure you are comfortable with the animal

As a helper, you need to feel comfortable around the animal that you will be working with. For example, if you have a slight fear of snakes, you may not be the best candidate for helping someone to overcome a snake phobia. If you have strong beliefs that dogs are dangerous, you may not be well suited to assist a person with overcoming a dog phobia. It is important for you to reflect on your own thoughts and feelings about the animal that you will be working with. If you are comfortable with the animal, then you may be well equipped to help with treatment.

In some cases, you may not be sure of how you feel about a certain animal because you have not had a lot of exposure to it yourself. For example, even if you don't have a strong fear of spiders, you may feel disgusted or unsure about the idea of holding one. In this case, you may want to practice on your own with the animal to see if you are able to get more comfortable before agreeing to be a helper. This is important because part of your role will be modeling nonfearful coping behaviors with the animal. You may need to touch or hold the animal if it is safe to do so. As you encounter and work with the animal in a nonfearful way, the person you are helping will become less anxious and will learn that it is possible to become more comfortable around the animal.

discuss your role as a helper up front

Each person with an animal phobia will have different needs or preferences. It is important to discuss these needs up front so that you know what is expected from you. One person may find encouragement during an exposure practice helpful, whereas another person may find supportive comments pushy or distracting. Some questions to ask the person you are helping include:

- ◊ "Do you have any concerns about this treatment approach that we could discuss?"

- ◊ "How can I help you prepare for your exposure practices?"

- ◊ "Are there any materials that I can help you get?"

- ◊ "Can I assist you to develop your exposure hierarchy?"

◊ "How can I help you during the actual exposure practice? Would you like me to suggest when you might be ready to move on to the next step? Or would you like me to wait until you say it is time to move on?"

◊ "Is there anything I can do that you might find helpful during the exposure practice? Are there any particular questions that I can ask you, based on what you learned from practicing the cognitive strategies? Are there certain phrases that you would find helpful to hear during the exposure practice?"

◊ "How can we prepare for possible obstacles during the exposure practice?"

◊ "After we finish the exposure practice, would it be helpful to discuss how it went and what the next step will be?"

◊ "If you find that you are getting discouraged, how can I help to keep you motivated? For instance, are there particular reasons that you have for overcoming this fear which I could remind you of, if needed?"

◊ "Are there any things you definitely do not want me to do?"

◊ "Are there any things that you definitely do not want me to say?"

helper "dos"

Given that there are individual differences in how each person will respond, it is difficult for us to say what you should always do or what you should never do as a helper. However, we have tried to cover some of the helpful or unhelpful behaviors below in the form of dos and don'ts. What to do comes first.

◊ Be patient and supportive.

◊ Try to convey an accepting attitude (such as, "It is okay to be scared during exposure; that means that you are really targeting your fear").

◊ Remember the other person is in charge. It is up to the person you are helping to determine how far he or she will go in any practice.

◊ Try to be understanding and kind, even when an exposure seems to be taking a long time or when it seems hard to understand why it is so difficult for the person you are helping.

◊ Model nonfearful coping behavior when interacting with the animal (show that you feel comfortable and safe).

◊   If the person you are helping becomes dis-
     couraged, remind him or her of the gains
     that have been made so far.

◊   Set aside time to assist with exposures.
     Build the practices into your schedule.

◊   During exposure practices, check in with
     the person periodically to gauge his or her
     fear level on a scale from 0 (no fear) to 100
     (extreme fear).

◊   Gently encourage the person to continue
     with the next step in the exposure as he or
     she feels ready (depending on the fear level).
     For instance, a fear rating of 35 or below sug-
     gests a low level of fear and that continuing
     with the next step should be manageable for
     most people. A fear rating of 35 to 60
     suggests a moderate level of fear, a level at
     which many people are able to try something
     more difficult. A fear rating of 60 to 80
     suggests a high degree of fear and indicates
     that continuing with the next step in the
     exposure practice may be quite challenging
     and uncomfortable. A fear rating of 80 to
     100 signals an extreme level of fear, and pro-
     ceeding with the next step at this point may
     be very difficult and overwhelming. If it is too
     difficult, it may be a good idea to wait at the

current step until the person's fear is reduced to a level of 60 or lower before moving on.

◇ If the person finds it helpful, you may assist by encouraging him or her to vocalize fearful thoughts during the exposure. As the helper, you can ask how likely these predictions are to come true. You can also ask questions that will help the person view the situation more realistically. For example, in chapter 4, we illustrated how Sam's wife helped him overcome his dog phobia. As Sam tried to approach the dog during exposure, his wife asked Sam about the anxious thoughts he was having. Sam responded, "I'm afraid the dog will suddenly move and bite me." His wife responded with another question: "How likely is that to happen?" Sam responded, "I know this is a friendly dog that has never bitten anyone. The chances of him biting me today are extremely small." Sam's wife responded, "When you think about the actual chances of being bitten, does your level of fear change?" Sam nodded and said, "Yes, it really brings my fear down when I think that this dog is not dangerous." In this example, you can see that as a helper you can assist the person to become aware of his or her thoughts in the situation and to focus on using the strategies he or she has learned from following this book.

◊   Help the person to see the gains that he or she is making throughout the process. Even the smallest steps should be reinforced with positive feedback and encouragement. This feedback will provide the boost needed to continue working on exposures.

◊   If the person is getting down on him- or herself because progress isn't as quick as expected or because the exposures were harder then anticipated, you can remind him or her that it takes a lot of strength and courage to overcome a major fear. It may take some time to get over the fear, especially if it is particularly severe and longstanding. Encourage the person to take things one step at a time.

Here are some helpful phrases to use during exposure practices:

◊   "This fear will peak and then pass."

◊   "Each exposure step, no matter how small, is an important step toward overcoming your fear."

◊   "Exposure is tough. It is short-term pain for long-term gain."

◊ "Take things one step at a time. You can do it."

◊ "You are doing great. This is very hard work."

◊ "Ride your fear like a wave."

Here are some questions that may help during exposure practice:

◊ "What is the worst thing that could happen in this situation?"

◊ "If the worst thing does happen, how would you cope?"

◊ "What are the reasons you have for going through this process?"

◊ "Where is your fear level right now?"

◊ "Do you feel ready to move on to the next step?"

◊ "What strategies have you learned in the book that could help you in this situation?"

◊ "What anxious thoughts are you having right now?"

◊ "What evidence do you have that your anxious thoughts are true or not true?"

◊ "What is another way to view this situation?"

helper "don'ts"

Now, here are some behaviors to avoid:

◊   Do not trivialize the person's fear.

◊   Do not become angry or frustrated. If you do become frustrated, try to keep it to yourself and give yourself some time to unwind before the next exposure practice.

◊   Do not be pushy or impatient, even if things seem to be going very slowly. Plan for each exposure to take a few hours, so you don't feel stressed or rushed because you have other things to do.

◊   Don't force the person to stay in the situation if he or she decides to escape. Instead, provide support and encouragement to try again if possible.

◊   Do not act fearful or disgusted when interacting with the animal (for instance, don't scream or act repulsed when touching a spider or mouse). Displaying your fearful or negative reactions to the animal could cause an increase in the fear level of the person you are trying to help.

◊   Don't make jokes about the person's fear or the exposure practices. Take things seriously, even if the practices seem silly (for instance, practices that involve repeating the phrase "slithery snake" or trying to touch a picture of a mouse).

◊ When you are assisting the person to become aware of his or her anxious thoughts, do not give advice or feedback on how realistic you believe the thoughts are. Instead, use questions that will help the person come to a realistic conclusion after considering the evidence supporting the anxious thoughts as well as the evidence contradicting the thoughts (as illustrated above in the example of Sam and his wife).

Summary

This chapter discussed the important role that a helper may play in the recovery process. Being a helper requires making a commitment and making sure that you are comfortable with the animal. It is important to discuss your role as a helper up front so that you know what is expected and needed from you. This chapter also reviewed phrases or questions that may be beneficial as you assist someone to overcome his or her fear. Although the person you help is unique and will have individual needs and preferences, we have provided some definite dos and don'ts that may serve as useful guidelines for assisting someone to overcome his or her phobia.

references

American Psychiatric Association. 2000. *Diagnostic and Statistical Manual of Mental Disorders.* 4th ed. Text revision. Washington, D.C.: American Psychiatric Association.

Antony, M. M., and D. H. Barlow. 2002. Specific phobia. In *Anxiety and Its Disorders: The Nature and Treatment of Anxiety and Panic* 2nd ed. edited by D. H. Barlow. New York: Guilford Press.

Antony, M. M., T. A. Brown, and D. H. Barlow. 1997. Heterogeneity among specific phobia types in DSM-IV. *Behaviour Research and Therapy* 35: 1089–1100.

Antony, M. M., and R. P. Swinson. 2000. *Phobic Disorders and Panic in Adults: A Guide to Assessment and*

Treatment. Washington, D.C.: American Psychological Association.

Bourdon, K. H., J. H. Boyd, D. S. Rae, B. J. Burns, J. W. Thompson, and B. Z. Locke. 1988. Gender differences in phobias: Results of the ECA community study. *Journal of Anxiety Disorders* 2:227–241.

Car-accidents.com. Get the facts: Statistics. http://www.car-accidents.com/pages/stats.html.

Curtis, G. C., W. J. Magee, W. W. Eaton, H. U. Wittchen, and R. C. Kessler. 1998. Specific fears and phobias: Epidemiology and classification. *British Journal of Psychiatry* 173:212–217.

Davey, C. L., L. Forster, and G. Mayhew. 1993. Familial resemblances in disgust sensitivity and animal phobias. *Behaviour Research and Therapy* 31:41–50.

de Jong, P. J., H. Andrea, and P. Muris. 1997. Spider phobia in children: Disgust and fear before and after treatment. *Behaviour Research and Therapy* 35:559–562.

Fyer, A. J., S. Mannuzza, M. S. Gallops, L. Y. Martin, C. Aaronson, J. G. Gorman, M. R. Liebowitz, and D. F. Klein. 1990. Familial transmission of simple phobias and fears. *Archives of General Psychiatry* 47: 252–256.

Harris. C. Spider bites. http://www.marion.ohio-state.edu/spiderweb/spider%20bites.htm.

Hellström, K., and L. G. Öst. 1995. One-session therapist directed exposure vs. two forms of manual directed self-exposure in the treatment of spider phobia. *Behaviour Research and Therapy* 33:959–965.

Jones, M. K., S. Whitmont, and R. G. Menzies. 1996. Danger expectancies and insight in spider phobia. *Anxiety* 2:179–185.

Kendler, K. S., L. M. Karkowski, and C. A. Prescott. 1999. Fear and phobias: Reliability and heritability. *Psychological Medicine* 29:539–553.

Merckelbach, H., A. Arntz, W. A. Arrindell, and P. J. de Jong. 1992. Pathways to spider phobia. *Behaviour Research and Therapy* 30:543–546.

Merckelbach, H., P. J. de Jong, A. Arntz, and E. Schouten. 1993. The role of evaluative learning and disgust sensitivity in the etiology and treatment of spider phobia. *Advances in Behaviour Research and Therapy* 15:243–255.

National Center for Injury Prevention and Control. Ten leading causes of nonfatal injury. United States, 2002. http://www.cdc. gov/ncipc/osp/charts.htm.

National Marine Fisheries Service. NOAA Fisheries Fact Sheet. http://www.nmfs.noaa.gov/sharks/FS_faq.htm.

Öst, L. G. 1989. One-session treatment for specific phobias. *Behaviour Research and Therapy* 27:1–7.

Öst, L. G. 1996. Long-term effects of behavior therapy for specific phobia. In *Long-Term Treatments of the Anxiety Disorders*, edited by M. R. Mavissakalian and R. F. Prien. Washington, D.C.: American Psychiatric Press.

Öst, L. G., P. M. Salkovskis, and K. Hellström. 1991. One-session therapist directed exposure vs. self-exposure in the treatment of spider phobia. *Behavior Therapy* 22:407–422.

Öst, L. G., B. M. Stridh, and M. Wolf. 1998. A clinical study of spider phobia: Prediction of outcome after self-help and therapist-directed treatments. *Behaviour Research and Therapy* 36:17–35.

Paralumun New Age Women's Village. American rape statistics. http://www.paralumun.com/issuesrapestats.htm.

Phillips, K. M. 1999. Dog bite law. http://www.dogbite law.com.

Pierce, K. A., and D. R. Kirkpatrick. 1992. Do men lie on fear surveys? *Behaviour Research and Therapy* 30:415–418.

Poulton, R., and R. G. Menzies. 2002. Non-associative fear acquisition: A review of the evidence from retrospective and longitudinal research. *Behaviour Research and Therapy* 40:127–149.

Rachman, S. 1977. The conditioning theory of fear-acquisition: A critical examination. *Behaviour Research and Therapy* 15:375–387.

Rachman, S., and M. Cuk. 1992. Fearful distortions. *Behaviour Research and Therapy* 30:583–589.

Riskind, J. H., R. Moore, and L. Bowley. 1995. The looming of spiders: The fearful perceptual distortion of movement and menace. *Behaviour Research and Therapy* 33:171–178.

Seligman, M. E. P. 1971. Phobias and preparedness. *Behavior Therapy* 2:307–320.

Thorpe, S. J., and P. M. Salkovskis. 1998. Selective attention to real phobic and safety stimuli. *Behaviour Research and Therapy* 36:471–481.

UniSci International Science News. 2002. Falling coconuts kill more people than shark attacks. May 23. http://unisci.com/stories/20022/0523024.htm.

University of Maryland Medical System. 2003. Unintentional injury statistics. http//www.umm.edu/non_trauma/stats.htm.

Wessel, I., and H. Merckelbach. 1998. Memory for threat-relevant and threat-irrelevant cues in spider phobics. *Cognition and Emotion* 12:93–104.

Woody, S. R., and B. A. Teachman. 2000. Intersection of disgust and fear: Normative and pathological views. *Clinical Psychology: Science and Practice* 7:291–311.

Martin M. Antony, Ph.D. is professor in the Department of Psychiatry and Behavioural Neurosciences at McMaster University. He is also director of the Anxiety Treatment and Research Centre and psychologist-in-chief at St. Joseph's Healthcare in Hamilton, Ontario. He received his Ph.D. in clinical psychology from the University at Albany, State University of New York, and completed his predoctoral internship training at the University of Mississippi Medical Center in Jackson, MS. He has published fourteen books and more than one hundred scientific papers and book chapters in the areas of cognitive behavior therapy and anxiety disorders. He has received early career awards from the Society of Clinical Psychology (American Psychological Association), the Canadian Psychological Association, and the Anxiety Disorders Association of America, and is a fellow of the American and Canadian Psychological Associations. He is past president of the Anxiety Disorders Special Interest Group of the Association for Advancement of Behavior Therapy (AABT) and has been program chair for the AABT annual convention. He is actively involved in clinical research in the area of anxiety disorders, teaching and education, and maintains a clinical practice. His Web site may be found at **www.martinantony.com**.

Randi McCabe, Ph.D. is Chair of the Clinical Behavioural Sciences Programme in the Faculty of Health Sciences and assistant professor in the Department of Psychiatry and Behavioural Neurosciences at McMaster University. She is also associate director of the Anxiety Treatment and Research Centre at St. Joseph's Healthcare in Hamilton, Ontario. After receiving her Ph.D. in psychology from the University of Toronto, she completed pre-doctoral internship training in the Eating Disorder Program at the Toronto General Hospital. She has published numerous scientific papers and book chapters in the areas of cognitive behavior therapy, anxiety disorders, and eating disorders. She is the lead author of *Overcoming Bulimia: A Step-by-Step Cognitive Behavioral Workbook*, and is a coauthor on *10 Simple Solutions to Panic: How to Overcome Panic Attacks, Calm Physical Symptoms, and Reclaim Your Life*. She is on the editorial board of *The Clinical Psychologist* and has been assistant chair of the Program Committee for the Association for Advancement of Behavior Therapy (AABT) annual convention. She is actively involved in clinical research, teaching, and education. She also maintains a private practice.

Some Other New Harbinger Titles

Angry All the Time, Item 3929 $13.95

Handbook of Clinical Psychopharmacology for Therapists, 4th edition, Item 3996 $55.95

Writing For Emotional Balance, Item 3821 $14.95

Surviving Your Borderline Parent, Item 3287 $14.95

When Anger Hurts, 2nd edition, Item 3449 $16.95

Calming Your Anxious Mind, Item 3384 $12.95

Ending the Depression Cycle, Item 3333 $17.95

Your Surviving Spirit, Item 3570 $18.95

Coping with Anxiety, Item 3201 $10.95

The Agoraphobia Workbook, Item 3236 $19.95

Loving the Self-Absorbed, Item 3546 $14.95

Transforming Anger, Item 352X $10.95

Don't Let Your Emotions Run Your Life, Item 3090 $17.95

Why Can't I Ever Be Good Enough, Item 3147 $13.95

Your Depression Map, Item 3007 $19.95

Successful Problem Solving, Item 3023 $17.95

Working with the Self-Absorbed, Item 2922 $14.95

The Procrastination Workbook, Item 2957 $17.95

Coping with Uncertainty, Item 2965 $11.95

The BDD Workbook, Item 2930 $18.95

You, Your Relationship, and Your ADD, Item 299X $17.95

The Stop Walking on Eggshells Workbook, Item 2760 $18.95

Call **toll free, 1-800-748-6273,** or log on to our online bookstore at **www.newharbinger.com** to order. Have your Visa or Mastercard number ready. Or send a check for the titles you want to New Harbinger Publications, Inc., 5674 Shattuck Ave., Oakland, CA 94609. Include $4.50 for the first book and 75¢ for each additional book, to cover shipping and handling. (California residents please include appropriate sales tax.) Allow two to five weeks for delivery.

Prices subject to change without notice.